International Dollhouses and Accessories 1880s to 1980s

Dian Zillner

4880 Lower Valley Road, Atglen, PA 19310 USA

Dedication

Dedicated to Gail Carey and Roy Specht, fellow collectors
who have become good friends through our association with
dollhouse collecting and the dollhouse books.

Notice: All of the items in this book are from private collections and museums. Grateful acknowledgment is made to the original producers of the materials photographed. The copyright has been identified for each item whenever possible. If any omission or incorrect information is found, please notify the author or publisher and it well be amended in any future edition of the book.

The prices listed in these captions are intended only as a guide, and should not be used to set prices for dollhouses and related products. Prices vary from one section of the country to another and also from dealer to dealer. The prices listed here are the best estimates the author can give at the time of publication but prices in the field can change quickly. This is especially true with the added sales from the Internet. Neither the author nor the publisher assumes responsibility for any losses that might be incurred as a result of consulting this price guide.

Front cover (clockwise from top left): Brumberger Colonial House, circa 1975; C. Moritz Reichel dollhouse, circa 1930s. *Courtesy of Patty Cooper*; Handmade dollhouse, circa early 1900s; Moritz Gottschalk dollhouse, circa early 1900s. *Courtesy of Ruth Petros*; Moritz Gottschalk red roof "stucco" house, circa 1930. *Courtesy of Dollhouse and Miniature Museum of Cape May*; Handmade dollhouse, circa early 1900s.

Back cover (bottom left to right): Lithographed paper over wood dollhouse. *Courtesy of Leslie and Joanne Payne*; Lithographed paper over wood dollhouse, circa 1900-1910.

Library of Congress Cataloging-in-Publication Data

Zillner, Dian.
    International dollhouses and accessories, 1880s to 1980s/by Dian Zillner.
        p. cm.
    ISBN 0-7643-1725-3
    1. Dollhouses--Collectors and collecting--Catalogs. 2. Dollhouses--History--19th century--Catalogs. 3. Dollhouses--History--20th century--Catalogs. 4. Doll furniture--Collectors and collecting--Catalogs. 5. Doll furniture--History--19th century--Catalogs. 6. Doll furniture--History--20th century--Catalogs. I. Title.
    NK4893.Z55 2003
    745.592'3'075--dc21
                        2002156716

"Schiffer," "Schiffer Publishing Ltd. & Design," and the "Design of pen and ink well" are registered trademarks of Schiffer Publishing Ltd.
Designed by "Sue"
Type set in Lydian BT/Souvenir Lt BT
ISBN: 0-7643-1725-3
Printed in China
1 2 3 4

Published by Schiffer Publishing Ltd.
4880 Lower Valley Road
Atglen, PA 19310
Phone: (610) 593-1777; Fax: (610) 593-2002
E-mail: Info@schifferbooks.com
Please visit our web site catalog at **www.SCHIFFERBOOKS.COM**
We are always looking for people to write books on new and related subjects. If you have an idea for a book, please contact us at the above address.

This book may be purchased from the publisher.
Include $3.95 for shipping.
Please try your bookstore first.
You may write for a free catalog.

In Europe, Schiffer books are distributed by
Bushwood Books
6 Marksbury Avenue
Kew Gardens
Surrey TW9 4JF England
Phone: 44 (0) 20 8392 8585
Fax: 44 (0) 20 8392 9876
E-mail: Bushwd@aol.com
Free postage in the UK. Europe: air mail at cost.

Contents

Introduction and Acknowledgments 4

Chapter 1: Furnished Dollhouses 5

Chapter 2: Cardboard and Paper Dollhouses and Furniture 129

Chapter 3: American Dollhouses and Furniture 152

Chapter 4: English Dollhouses and Furniture 188

Chapter 5: German Dollhouses and Furniture 201

Chapter 6: Japanese Dollhouse and Furniture 221

Chapter 7: Display 233

Bibliography 241

Index 243

Introduction and Acknowledgments

After completing four books dealing with dollhouses and other toy buildings (two with co-author Patty Cooper), the author planned to end her part in this series of books. However, it wasn't long after *Furnished Dollhouses 1880s-1980s* went to the publisher that collectors began to find new information on various dollhouses and furniture. After consulting with earlier contributors, it was decided to add another book to the series. These collectors also agreed with the decision to make this book primarily a picture book. Collectors who want more information about the various companies responsible for the production of most of the dollhouses and their furnishings should refer to the "Companies" section in *Furnished Dollhouses 1880s-1980s* (see Bibliography). Additional firms were covered in *Antique and Collectible Dollhouses and Their Furnishings* (with Patty Cooper) and *American Dollhouses and Furniture From the 20th Century*. The captions in this book identify the company and date of production for the item whenever possible. More information is provided for firms that have not been covered before.

Because of the popularity of *Furnished Dollhouses 1880s-1980s*, the first part of this book uses the same format as that one. Although companies are listed in chronological order, few companies who made the products pictured were in business for only one decade. In those cases, the firm was placed in the decade in which *most* of the illustrated products were produced.

The rest of this book includes an extensive chapter on cardboard and paper dollhouses and furniture plus updates and additions to houses and furniture made in America, England, and Germany. New to this book is a chapter on Japan's contribution to the miniature world. It is hoped that with the addition of this book, collectors will have even more information to help them in the identification of their houses and furniture.

A short chapter on "Display" has been added to this book to provide collectors with ideas on how to display collections in their homes. As in previous books, a price guide and bibliography are also included.

Several collectors and good friends have been on hand to help with all the dollhouse books from the very beginning. They have always been kind enough to offer support, pictures, information, and, in Gail Carey's, case needed repair whenever asked. It's impossible to determine how many pictures Roy Specht has taken or how many telephone consultations Patty Cooper has contrib-

uted to make the books possible. Marcie Tubbs and Marilyn Pittman have also supplied pictures and information for each of the books and their friendship is also highly valued. More recent acquaintances, Ruth Petros and Becky Norris, have been on board in a big way beginning with the second book. Through frequent phone calls, friendships have grown. Again, a special "thank you" to Marge Meisinger for sharing her great catalog collection so many vintage advertisements could be pictured.

The author expresses appreciation to the many other individuals who answered questions, shared materials, and took photographs in order to make this book possible. Included are: Sharon Barton; Linda Boltrek; Gordon Blaker at the Augusta, Georgia Museum of History; Samm Burnham; Liz Cathcart; Jeff Carey; Ray Carey; Lois Freeman; Rita Goranson; Bonnie B. Hanson; Mary Harris; Gillian and John Kernon; Judith and Gary Mosholder; George Mundorf; Arliss and Gene Morris; Marge Powell; Elaine Price; Marianne Price; Nancy Roeder; Marian Schmuhl; Susan Singer; Evangeline Steinmeier; Karen Steinmeier; Mary and Werner Stuecher; Marguerite Sweeney; Bob Tubbs; Mary Lu and Bob Trowbridge; Harry Vaden; Shirley C. Parks, Curator of Winchendon Historical Society, Home of Toy Museum of Converse and Mason & Parker Toys; and to dealers Ann Meehan, (603) 433-5650, antkdh@attbi.com; and Leslie and Joanne Payne, (315) 637-6484. Thanks also to the following dollhouse museums: The Toy and Miniature Museum of Kansas City (816) 333-2055; Libby Goodman and The Dollhouse and Miniature Museum of Cape May, New Jersey (609) 884-6371; Carol Stevenson and the Mineral Point Toy Museum in Mineral Point, Wisconsin (608) 987-3160; and a special thanks to Eleanor LaVove, Jackie McMahan, and Karen Griffiths of Angel's Attic in Santa Monica, California (310) 394-8331 for allowing us to photograph several of their houses.

Special recognition goes to members of my family who were so helpful in the preparation of this book. To my daughter, Suzanne Silverthorn, who once again was my photographer; and to my son, Jeff Zillner, who, as always, helped with some editing.

Acknowledgment and extra recognition is also extended to Schiffer Publishing Ltd. and its excellent staff, particularly to Sue Taylor, designer, and Donna Baker, editor, who helped with this publication. Without their support and extra effort, this book would not have been possible.

Chapter 1
Furnished Dollhouses

Because of the interest shown by collectors in the *Furnished Dollhouses 1880s-1980s* book, the author is pleased to be able to picture more dollhouses in their most collectible form: furnished with the appropriate furniture and accessories.

1880s and Earlier

Handmade Houses

Unlike most houses, this nineteenth century house opens like a book to reveal its six rooms. The current owner has chosen to furnish the house as three rooms with each of its three floors used as one room. The inside of the house has also been redecorated. The rooms have been furnished as a dining room, parlor, and bedroom-children's room. *Dollhouse and Miniature Museum of Cape May.*

Handmade dollhouse, circa 1870s to 1880s, thought to be English. Although the house has been repainted, the architectural details are original ($9,000-10,000). 53" high x 41" wide x 20.5" deep. *Photographs and house from the collection of the Dollhouse and Miniature Museum of Cape May.*

A larger scale German Biedermeier settee (circa 1850-1860) with silk upholstery and a Biedermeier oval tea table (circa 1880s) set with treen wood dishes. The dollhouse soldier doll with a molded hat is all original. All of the items are from the right side of the dining room (settee $500-600, tea table $350-400, dishes $200+, doll $1,250). *Dollhouse and Miniature Museum of Cape May.*

The settee, tea table, treenware, and soldier doll are shown in the right side of the first floor room of the house. Both rooms on the first floor have matching fireplaces. *Dollhouse and Miniature Museum of Cape May.*

The room on the left side of the first floor dining room is also furnished with Biedermeier furniture. Besides a table and chairs, the furniture includes a marble topped sideboard. *Dollhouse and Miniature Museum of Cape May.*

The room on the right side of the second floor parlor is furnished with a seven piece set of pressed tinplate furniture made by the German firm of Rock & Graner, circa 1875. *Dollhouse and Miniature Museum of Cape May.*

Four pieces of the German Rock & Graner parlor set pictured in the second floor room on the right. The pressed tinplate set was made circa 1875 (seven piece set $3,500-4,000). *Dollhouse and Miniature Museum of Cape May.*

The left side of the parlor features a china head "painter" working on a portrait of a china head doll dressed in pink. All of the dolls are German. The "painter" has a desirable and unusual hair style. Notice the matching fireplaces in the two sides of the parlor as well as the mirrors and figurines used as accessories. *Dollhouse and Miniature Museum of Cape May.*

Biedermeier chair with upholstered seat and arm rests in an oversized scale circa 1860 and a German china head all original doll used as the painter in the parlor (chair $250, doll $400-500). *Dollhouse and Miniature Museum of Cape May.*

The room in the right side of the third floor features the children who live in the house along with their toys. The all-bisque German dolls (circa 1910-1920s) have molded hair, painted features, and jointed arms and legs. A German china head "nanny" looks after the children (bisque dolls $100-150 each, toys $50-100 each). *Dollhouse and Miniature Museum of Cape May.*

The inside of Eaton Place contains four rooms that still retain their original wallpaper. The house has been furnished as a parlor, dining room, and two bedrooms. Most of the furniture is German Biedermeier. *Angel's Attic Collection, Jeff Carey photograph.*

Handmade wood house called Eaton Place. It is dated 1864 on the back along with the initials of the original owner. It was made in Falmouth, England by a builder for his year old granddaughter. The child's portrait hangs in the house (not enough examples to determine price). 39" high (not including chimneys) x 40" wide x 17" deep. The front steps are 13.5" wide by 4" deep. *House courtesy of Angel's Attic. Photographs by Jeff Carey.*

Right:
The parlor is located on the lower left of the house. It includes an original fireplace. The room has been furnished with a German Biedermeier parlor set that includes a sofa and four chairs. A unique desk, cabinet, and marble topped tea table are also Biedermeier pieces. The room is full of interesting accessories including a bust of Queen Victoria, a globe in a stand, ormolu light fixture, three decorated china plates mounted on metal, and several pieces of Bristol glass. The dollhouse dolls living in the house include a soldier doll and his lady friend. *Angel's Attic Collection, Jeff Carey photograph.*

The dining room on the lower right is also furnished with German Biedermeier furniture. Included are a marble topped dining room table, two servers, hutch, and a cabinet. A unique wine holder is in the foreground of the room. The blue and white dishes are unmarked Chinese pieces. *Angel's Attic Collection, Jeff Carey photograph.*

The bedroom in the upstairs left also includes an original fireplace. It, too, is furnished with German Biedermeier furniture. Included are a bed, dresser, table, chairs, desk, and a tall cabinet with curtains mounted inside. Many of the pieces feature marble tops. A German china head doll lives in this room. Bristol glass adds colorful accents. *Angel's Attic Collection, Jeff Carey photograph.*

The bedroom on the right also features German Biedermeier furnishings. Bristol glass adds color to this room as well. Other accessories include antique wall light fixtures, a chandelier, sewing basket, mantel clock, and pictures on the wall. The picture on the right on the back wall is a painting of the original owner of the house with her mother. It was painted from a photograph by Catherine MacLaren, founder of the *Nutshell News* publication. *Angel's Attic Collection, Jeff Carey photograph.*

Fashion doll 6" tall wearing her antique clothing. She is pictured with a trunk full of accessories including a tin hand mirror, watch, combs, and purse. *Photograph and doll from the collection of Linda Boltrek.*

Large handmade "open front" nineteenth century house that came from Maine. The house was assembled using square nails. The outside retains its worn white paint with dark green trim around the four windows and base. The inside includes four rooms with old painted walls and floors. The rooms in the house have been furnished as a parlor, kitchen, and two bedrooms. The furniture is all large scale; most of it was really made to be used by dolls but the pieces work well in this large house ($4,000-5,000). 43" high x 48" wide x 21" deep. *Photographs and house from the collection of Susan Singer.*

The nicest piece featured in the kitchen of the large house is the iron cookstove that belonged to the owner's mother in 1915 ($300). It measures 11" wide x 7" tall. Other kitchen furnishings include a wood table and chairs and work table along with various accessories. A tea kettle, coal scuttle, pitchers, bowls, and a broom are all used in the house's kitchen. *Singer Collection.*

The parlor on the first floor features a camel back sofa, circa 1850, 13" long by 8.5" tall. It is covered in its original worn chintz and was probably handmade. Other furnishings include a large desk with drop front, upholstered rocking chair, and a wood rocker. All of the floors feature small hand braided rugs. *Singer Collection.*

The upstairs bedroom on the left features a bed, circa 1850, with a horsehair mattress (bed $300-400). The bed is 10" long x 9" tall. Other furnishings include a cradle, drop front desk, rocking chair, and washstand with pitcher. *Singer Collection.*

The bedroom on the right is furnished with a wood bedroom set painted cream with blue trim. The bed is 13" long x 8" tall. The set includes a dresser, high boy, bed, vanity, bench, chair and night stand. Accessories used in the room include a chamber pot, suitcase, mirrors, and a picture. *Singer Collection.*

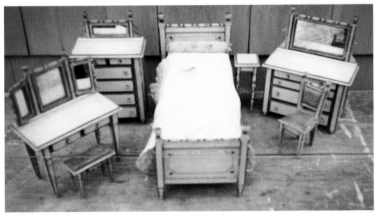

The interesting large scale bedroom set was originally made to be used with a regular doll but fits nicely in this large house. The drawers are functional. It is very unusual to find such a complete set. Doll furniture was usually sold by the piece instead of in sets (set $1,000+). *Singer Collection.*

Although no dolls currently inhabit this large house, these two all bisque jointed German dolls would fit nicely. Because they are 5" and 5.5" tall, they are too large in scale to be used in most doll houses. They would make nice children for a house this large. The dolls have glass eyes and applied wigs. They have been nicely redressed ($125-150 each). *Photograph by Suzanne Silverthorn.*

Early English nineteenth century box back house. The handmade house includes the original painted bricks on the outside along with interesting window trim. The house was assembled with square nails and its original hinges were made of leather (not enough examples to determine price). 23" high x 13" wide x 8" deep *From the collection of Leslie and Joanne Payne. Photograph by Leslie Payne.*

The front of the house opens to reveal the two rooms inside. Both of the rooms still retain their original wallpaper. The downstairs fireplace is original to the house. Two German china head dolls visit in the downstairs parlor. *Payne Collection.*

A lovely German china head doll is pictured in the upstairs. Her hair is molded in an unusual "Jenny Lind" style that makes her more desirable. *Payne Collection.*

The house has been furnished with German furniture and accessories. Included are a matching Biedermeier bed (with original bedding) and chair ($300-350), an English Evans & Cartwright metal fireplace, soft metal birdcage and stand ($175-200), an ormolu lamp ($150-175), and a very old chest made of brass and wood. *Payne Collection.*

Christian Hacker

The inside of the main part of the house can be accessed by opening two sections of the front of the house. The rooms on the third level can be reached by removing the top of the roof. The main part of the house has four large rooms and two halls. The staircase is in the hall. There is a built-in stove and cupboard in the kitchen. The house contains its original wallpapers and floor coverings. *Meehan Collection.*

German Christian Hacker dollhouse circa 1880s. This house is very typical of most of the houses made by the firm. It came in four pieces and can be assembled easily. The pieces include the first floor, the second floor, the attic or third floor, and the top part of the roof, which can also be removed. The house is painted creamy yellow with apricot trim. Raised quoining has been used on the ends of each side of the front of the house. The house has a curved balcony and a double front entrance ($10,000). 35.5" high x 31" wide x 16" deep. *Photograph and house from the collection of Ann Meehan.*

The built-in cupboard in the kitchen features a fine set of treen dishes, which are made of turned wood ($1,000). *Meehan Collection.*

Left:
The kitchen "staff" includes a cook with mutton chops ($600) and a black maid ($850). Both dollhouse dolls have bisque heads and lower limbs. Behind the maid is an unusual lava bowl with marbleized painting ($450). *Meehan Collection.*

Rare knife holder from the dining room of the Hacker house. The treen bowl is for fruit. The knives fit in the top ($395). *Meehan Collection.*

The downstairs hall features a Waltershausen (also known as Biedermeier) Gothic pier mirror ($450), a single globe chandelier ($250), and an ormolu table lamp with double torches ($195). *Meehan Collection.*

The Hacker dining room also features a Biedermeier china cabinet with blue interior paper ($600), a larger Biedermeier china cabinet ($700) filled with Bristol dishes ($175), and a Biedermeier key cabinet ($350). An ormolu clock with a pendulum ($150) has been placed on the larger china cabinet. *Meehan Collection.*

Left:
The dining room furniture includes a Biedermeier sideboard in ebony finish with ivory knobs and carved ivory columns. This piece has exceptional stenciling ($1,000). Placed in the sideboard are a Staffordshire duck, hen, and swan sitting on their nests ($250 each). Also pictured is a rare Biedermeier octagonal dining room table with fine stenciling ($1,200). *Meehan Collection.*

The parlor, located on the second floor right, has been furnished with a Biedermeier sofa and four chairs upholstered in rose flocked fabric (set $695). *Meehan Collection.*

The parlor also features this German Marklin fireplace ($550). The original wallpaper can be seen behind the fireplace. *Meehan Collection.*

Other interesting accessories in the parlor are a parrot on a stand ($195), a rare green porcelain lithophane (not enough examples to determine price), and an ormolu student lamp with a Bristol shade ($450). *Meehan Collection.*

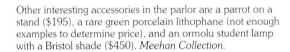

Other rare Biedermeier parlor furniture includes a round table that opens to insert leaves ($950), a whatnot shelf ($500), and a wall clock with a porcelain face ($350). *Meehan Collection.*

Unique Biedermeier handkerchief table located in the
Hacker parlor ($500). *Meehan Collection.*

This unusual ivory chess table is also housed in the parlor ($650).
Meehan Collection.

The upstairs hall in the Hacker house is filled with ormolu furniture and
accessories. Included are a birdcage ($295) and stand ($150), a chair ($195-
250), a console table with mirror, and a plant stand ($450) holding Austrian
Bronze flowers in pots ($50-75 each). *Meehan Collection.*

The upstairs bedroom is entirely furnished with ormolu furniture and
accessories. Pictured are an ormolu cradle ($500) and an ormolu chandelier
with electric bulbs and a center globe with a pink ruffle ($1,400). An unusual
dollhouse doll stands beside the cradle. Her head is of untinted bisque,
sometimes called Parian, and she wears a molded feather hat (not enough
examples to determine price). *Meehan Collection.*

Additional ormolu pieces used in the bedroom include a night stand ($250), standing mirror ($300), swag mirror ($950), and dressing table ($350). *Meehan Collection.*

Pictured in the bedroom of the Hacker house are an ormolu and asphaltum mirror with candle holders ($350), a matching shelf unit with mirror ($300), and an ormolu three tier shelf unit with candleholders on the sides ($800). *Meehan Collection.*

Four of the many dollhouse dolls, dressed in military uniforms, from the collection of Ann Meehan. The dolls are all original. They have bisque heads and all have molded hair and mustaches. *Meehan Collection.*

1890s

Mystery Houses

Wood house called "Mystery House" by collectors. A line of houses of this type was sold by F.A.O. Schwarz in the 1890s. The houses included unusual wood decorations on the outsides and unique woodwork around the windows. This is one of the larger versions of the house (not enough examples in this size to determine price). 50" high x 58" wide x 28" deep. *House courtesy of Angel's Attic. Photographs by Jeff Carey.*

The inside of the large Mystery House contains eight rooms (two could be considered halls). The house has been furnished as a kitchen, dining room, entry hall, parlor, two bedrooms, upstairs hall, and bathroom. Eight German dollhouse dolls live in the house, including a maid in the kitchen and a butler in the dining room. The house has been furnished mostly with German furniture, soft metal accessories, and ormolu framed pictures. *Angel's Attic Collection, Jeff Carey photograph.*

This "Mystery House" circa 1890s is in a small size not often seen ($5,000-8,000). 29" high x 25" wide x 15" deep. *From the collection of Leslie and Joanne Payne. Photographs by Leslie Payne.*

The inside of the smaller Mystery House contains four rooms furnished with German pieces in a small 1" to one foot scale. The rooms include a hall, dining room, bedroom, and parlor. The house features especially nice light fixtures including a wood treen chandelier in the upper left bedroom. The fixture is decorated with flowers like the treen dishes ($200+). The fixture in the lower left hall is a beaded one that has been electrified ($250-350). The hall furniture includes an ormolu birdcage, a Biedermeier desk, wind-up grandfather clock made of soft metal, brass, and tin, and a treen basket of flowers. *Payne Collection.*

The dining room has been furnished with golden oak furniture that includes a table, four chairs, and a matching sideboard with a marble top. The light fixture is made of soft metal and features a cupid decoration and tulip bulbs (fixture $200-350). Accessories include a glass fishbowl on an ormolu stand ($225-275) and an early treen tea set on the table. *Payne Collection.*

The parlor features a Biedermeier extension table and a five piece parlor set with cut velvet upholstery (sofa, three side chairs, and one arm chair $300+). Accessories include an ormolu light fixture with original shades ($400-500) and pictures with frames made of pressed cardboard. *Payne Collection*.

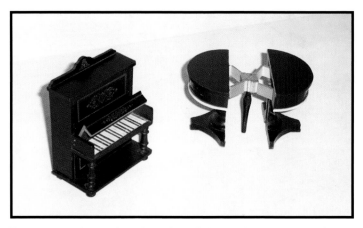

Two extra special pieces from the parlor include a Biedermeier piano with keyboard opening ($200-300) and a rare Biedermeier extension table (not enough examples to determine price). *Payne Collection*.

Interesting items from the bedroom include a Biedermeier sewing table ($200-250), a Biedermeier plant stand ($150-175), and a metal fireplace thought to have been made by the English firm of Evans & Cartwright ($300+). An ormolu lamp is displayed on the sewing table ($250-275). *Payne Collection*.

Larger Mystery House with gambrel roof and two doors in the front ($25,000). 44" high x 47" wide x 17" deep plus 8" for extension of front entrance. *Photograph and house from the collection of Ann Meehan.*

The front of the house opens in three sections to reveal six rooms. The house has been furnished as a parlor, dining room, and kitchen on the first floor, and a bedroom, nursery, and bathroom upstairs. The wallpaper and floor coverings are original. *Meehan Collection.*

The parlor (located in the lower left) is furnished with German Waltershausen furniture also known as Biedermeier in 1" to one foot to large 1" to one foot scale. An early china head doll with a "bald" head (as opposed to molded hair) and an applied wig stands beside a table. The light fixture, violin, picture, birdcage, candlesticks, and other antique German accessories add interest to the room. *Meehan Collection.*

This unusual Biedermeier parlor set from the Mystery House is Gothic in design. It includes one arm chair, four side chairs, and a sofa. All of the pieces are upholstered in flocked maroon velvet and gold (set $1,500). *Meehan Collection.*

Included in the Mystery House parlor furnishings are this rare Biedermeier Gothic pier mirror ($500) and German Marklin tin fireplace ($500). The Waltershausen pillow clock ($295) and the pair of Limoges vases ($110) add decor to the fireplace in the parlor. *Meehan Collection.*

The dining room is the middle room on the lower level of the Mystery House. It contains a rare set of furniture with ormolu mounted trim. The table and desk in the house have cabriole legs of metal with ormolu trim. A dollhouse doll with a china head and an unusual hair style shares the room with a dollhouse man who has a bisque head and glass eyes (set of sofa, four chairs, table, and desk $4,800). *Meehan Collection.*

A fine set of Treen wooden dishes is displayed in the dining room. They are painted blue and decorated with white flowers. The set also includes very rare matching triple candelabras in asphaltum (set $1,500). *Meehan Collection.*

One of the kitchen treasures is this rare set of tin canisters in two sizes with a double shelf that displays them nicely (set $1,500). Also pictured in the kitchen are a tin pie safe ($300) and a tin ice box ($495). All of the items are in blue and white. *Meehan Collection.*

Other accessories from the dining room include a bird cage mounted on an ormolu base ($700), unusual glass-eyed bisque dollhouse man in original suit and top hat ($1,400), and two highly decorative ormolu Art Nouveau mirrors ($295 each). *Meehan Collection.*

The Mystery House kitchen is furnished in tin, using pieces by the German Marklin or Bing firms, all in a blue and white color scheme. The soft metal "kerosene" chandelier was made in Germany and features a large Bristol glass globe. *Meehan Collection.*

Other interesting kitchen accessories include a tin ice water cooler on the wall ($400), a tin blue and white onion holder ($125), and tin flour and salt containers ($125 each). *Meehan Collection.*

The Mystery House bedroom is located in the upper left of the house. It is mostly furnished in German Biedermeier furniture, including a secretary desk with a great interior. In addition, there is an unusual Marklin bed with side panels ($2,900) and a rare Marklin chandelier with electric bulbs and a hanging globe in the center ($1,800). Two very unusual dolls are also shown in the room. They include a priest doll with a china head and limbs. He has a bald head with a painted area on top ($1,000). The dollhouse lady has a very fine untinted bisque head, an unusual hair style, and pierced ears. This type of doll head is sometimes called "Parian" by collectors ($650). *Meehan Collection.*

The Mystery House nursery is the middle room on the second floor. It features many pieces of rare German dollhouse furniture. Included is the Biedermeier cradle in the foreground ($500), the white Marklin metal bed with sides that come down ($1,500), Biedermeier armoire with stenciling ($400), and wardrobe with mirror ($400). The soft metal "kerosene" chandelier with beaded shade is also special ($650). *Meehan Collection.*

This fancy German soft metal carriage with pale blue lining ($395) and the soft metal cradle with lace drapery ($695) are also important pieces located in the nursery. *Meehan Collection.*

The nursery also houses some very unique German accessories. Included are a kerosene styled lamp ($450), a large ormolu mirror ($250), a photograph album in red leather ($400), an ivory double inkwell with candlesticks ($295), and a Biedermeier wash stand ($295). *Meehan Collection.*

Dollhouse lady doll 6" tall with untinted bisque (Parian) head. She has an unusual molded hair style with a molded band across the front. Her ears are pierced, which also adds to her rarity ($700-750). *Meehan Collection.*

Unusual 5.25" tall dollhouse doll with untinted bisque head (Parian type), circa 1870s, wearing a molded feather trimmed hat (not enough examples to determine price). *Meehan Collection.*

Handmade Houses

The front of the house opens in two parts to reveal four rooms and two halls. The rooms have been furnished as a kitchen, living room, bedroom, and dining room. Many pieces of furniture and also accessories used to furnish the house were "handmade" in America. *Price Collection.*

New Jersey "Red Brick" house, circa 1890. The handmade house was purchased at an estate sale in Orange, New Jersey a number of years ago. The house is displayed on a table that the present owner had made for it. There is a working lock on the front door and a working doorbell. A little trap door opens on the roof to access space where the battery for the doorbell was once stored. The doorbell has been rewired so that it works off the same wiring that powers the lights ($3,500). 49.5" high (excluding chimneys) x 39" wide x 26" deep. *Photographs and house from the collection of Marianne Price.*

The kitchen retains its original oilcloth on the floor and its curtains are also original to the house. The "Rival" cast iron stove is American. The green drop-leaf table is handmade, circa 1890. On the right side of the room is a metal German Rock and Graner cupboard, circa 1850-60. In the foreground a cat and mouse fight over a container of Camembert cheese that has fallen on the floor. *Price Collection.*

Handmade American Pine Chippendale sofa with bolsters, circa 1850 ($300), golfer dollhouse doll, and Victorian beadwork rug (rug $50). *Price Collection.*

The parlor is located on the lower left of the house. Featured on the left wall is a handmade early American Pine Chippendale sofa with bolsters, circa 1850. On the right wall is a large-scale Biedermeier Gothic desk. The owner, Marianne Price, made the needlepoint Heriz oriental carpet on the floor. Above the fireplace is an original oil painting of the White Mountains. On the wall above the sofa is a picture that is Victorian beadwork, circa 1840. The male doll is wearing his original gray suit with a red cravat. *Price Collection.*

Original oil painting of the White Mountains from the parlor accessories ($650). *Price Collection.*

Rare Biedermeier Gothic desk used in the parlor furnishings ($650). *Price Collection.*

Victorian beadwork picture from the parlor. It was originally half of a book cover. The "frame" is leather ($100). *Price Collection.*

The dining room is located in the upper left of the house. The table and chairs, sideboard, mirror, and knife boxes are handmade items. The chairs are copies of Biedermeier chairs. On the dining room table is a pair of Meyer sterling silver candlesticks with smoke chimneys. These were made in Newark, New Jersey, circa 1940. All the dolls in this room are dressed in their original clothing. *Price Collection.*

The bedroom contains three pieces (bed, chest of drawers, and night table) of handmade American fretwork furniture that came out of the Atlanta Toy Museum when it closed (set $650). On the floor is a Victorian beadwork rug. A handmade quilt hangs on the quilt rack. *Price Collection.*

Handmade American sideboard and matching knife boxes used in the dining room. The cloth on the sideboard dates to 1840 and is decorated with a pink and blue embroidered design consisting entirely of French knots. Also pictured is a pair of Meyer sterling silver candlesticks with smoke chimneys (sideboard, knife boxes and cloth $425, candlesticks $400). *Price Collection.*

Handmade American fretwork bedroom furniture used in the bedroom of the house ($650). *Price Collection.*

The unusual pantry can be accessed through its front door. The shelves were designed to hold kitchen or dining room supplies and accessories. *Burnham Collection, Singer photograph.*

Handmade large scale wood house, circa 1890. The outside of the house retains its original paint (yellow with green windows and mustard color roof and base). The right side of the house is decorated with two glass windows while the left side includes only one glass window on the upper floor. A pantry with shelves is on the left side of the house. The pantry is accessible from the front or from the dining room ($5,000+). 60" tall x 48" wide x 22" deep. *From the collection of Samm Burnham. Photographs by Susan Singer.*

The front of the house opens in two sections to reveal four rooms. The rooms have been furnished as a dining room, living room, and two bedrooms. The furniture is approximately 1 1/4" to one foot in scale. Included is an unidentified blue wood dining room set decorated with tiny flowers that matches the bedroom set pictured in a handmade house in the 1930s section. Both sets probably date from the 1920s. The wallpaper in the house appears to be original and the window coverings are also very old. *Burnham Collection, Singer photograph.*

1900s

Whitney Reed

The inside of the house contains two rooms papered in very old wallpaper which may be original. It is furnished with "Fairy" soft metal furniture made by Adrian Cooke Metallic Works of Chicago, Illinois, circa 1893. The bottom of the bed is marked "Pat. May 9, 1893." The furniture is 1/2" to one foot in scale. The gold metal hat rack was made in France. The small china doll is old while the other accessories are of recent origin (bed $65-75, rest of set $100+, hat rack $35-40).

Whitney S. Reed lithographed paper over wood house, circa 1898. The firm, based in Leominster, Massachusetts, produced some dollhouse furniture as well as dollhouses. This house has cut-out windows on the second floor while the first floor windows are printed paper. The front door is functional and the chimney is not original ($1,000-1,200). 11.5" high x 7.5" wide by 7" deep.

Label that came with the set of "Fairy" furniture (not including the bed). It states that the furniture was made of "An Alloy of Aluminum and White Metal." The manufacturer is listed as Adrian Cooke Metallic Works of Chicago, Illinois.

Whitney S. Reed lithographed paper over wood dollhouse, circa 1897-1898. The two-room house came with four glass windows, curtains, and an opening front door (not enough examples to determine price). 18" high to the top of tower x 7.25" wide x 3.75" deep (not including stairs). *Courtesy of Angel's Attic. Photograph by Jeff Carey.*

Unidentified Lithographed Houses

Lithographed paper over wood house probably made by the German Gottschalk firm for the French market, circa 1900. The decorative railing and tower roof have been replaced ($800-1,000). 22" high x 13" wide x 8.5" deep.

The inside of the house contains two rooms papered with what appears to be the original wallpapers. The house has been furnished with the type of German wood and upholstered furniture that has been found tied inside these houses when found MIB. The old accessories in the house include pressed brass framed pictures ($100+ each), metal lamp with glass globe ($100-125), the original mirror and clock attached to the matching fireplace, and the German dollhouse dolls who live in the house. The larger 6.75" doll has painted features and an applied wig ($200-250). The little girl is 4.75" tall and has molded hair along with painted features ($150-175).

Set of German furniture often used to furnish the German houses made for the French market. Included in this set were a fireplace with a brass framed clock and mirror, sofa, two side chairs, armchair and table (set $550-600). The furniture is 1" to one foot in scale.

Little girl German dollhouse dolls are hard to find. These dolls both have molded hair and painted features with bisque shoulder heads and lower limbs. The bodies and upper limbs on both dolls are cloth. They have been nicely dressed (3.5" and 4.75" tall, $135-175 each).

Unidentified lithographed paper over wood dollhouse, circa 1900-1910. The house has one dormer on the side of the roof, four cut-out windows, and a front door that opens. The lithographed colors are very bright on this house ($1,100-1,200). 17.5" high x 10.5" wide x 7.5" deep.

The inside of the lithographed house includes two rooms. Although the wallpaper is old, it is not original to the house. It has been furnished with small scale wood furniture (trimmed with decorated paper and fringe) and metal pieces made in France. The 3" dollhouse doll is white bisque with painted features and a wig.

The German parlor set includes a cabinet, table, sofa, and two chairs in a small 3/4" to one foot scale (set $50-75).

Metal pieces used in the house include a rocker, hat rack, and collapsible stroller, all made in France. The small German white bisque figure fits the stroller perfectly (metal pieces $40-45 each, figure $15+).

Handmade Houses

Dollhouse, thought to be handmade, circa early 1900s. This very well-made house has a "brick" foundation and chimney with lines cut in the wood to indicate bricks. The windows are glass and there is an unusual "stencil" design above the porch. The front porch includes railings and porch posts. The house is supposed to have been the childhood dollhouse of an elderly lady who used to invite neighborhood children to her home for tea parties many years ago. While visiting, the children were allowed to see and touch the dollhouse and its contents ($750). 22.5" high (not including chimney), x 21.5" wide x 14" deep including porch.

The front of the house opens to reveal three rooms and a staircase. It is still papered with the original wall and floor papers. The curtains are also original to the house. The furniture that came with the house includes the porch pieces, bedroom set, candy box cardboard piano, and the wood accessories on the serving cart. The other furniture has been added. The house contains old commercially made floor papers and small scale commercial wallpapers. Perhaps it was produced in a cottage industry setting many years ago.

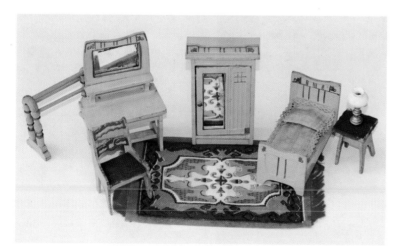

German bedroom furniture in a 3/4" to small 1" to one foot scale that was in the house when it was purchased by the present owner. The dresser and quilt rack are in a larger scale than the other pieces. The bedroom chairs match the German chairs and other furniture used to furnish the dining room and living room (set $100).

Soft metal German stove in a large 3/4" to one foot scale used in the living room ($50).

Large handmade wood house from 1903. The house has a mansard roof, upstairs and downstairs porches, and old green slag glass in the top panes of many of the windows. The other parts of the windows have been covered with a lightly patterned paper to look like old glass. The chimney is probably a replacement. This house was once in the collection of Catherine MacLaren (early editor and publisher of *Nutshell News*). The house has been redecorated. On the bottom of the house is inscribed "Merry Christmas, 1903" ($900-1,100). 33" high (not including chimney) x 29" wide x 24.5" deep.

When the front of the house is opened, four large rooms are revealed. The inside of the house has also been redecorated. The rooms have been furnished as a kitchen, parlor, bedroom, and nursery.

The living room, as well as the entire house, has been furnished with larger scale furniture ranging from 1.25" to 1.5" to one foot in scale. The dolls are also in the larger scale. The German baby rests in her metal German buggy (picture on back wall $125+).

The German upholstered living room set includes a sofa, four side chairs, and a table. The old German metal clock and the 1890 calendar advertising Colgate and Co. decorate the top of the table. Two all bisque jointed German boy dolls play with their toys in the parlor. The dolls are 4.75" and 5" tall. Both have painted features and molded hair (parlor set $225-275, calendar $25, dolls $75-100 each, clock $40).

Other pieces from the parlor include an English Evans & Cartwright tinplate table, a large scale brass and glass lamp, and a tall metal statue with an attached mirror. The tin heating stove comes from the bedroom and is 5.75" tall (table $200+ [with mended leg], lamp $100-125, statue $100-125, heating stove $100-125).

The kitchen furnishings include an iron cookstove, wood kitchen cabinet, and a high chair, as well as the items pictured. Included are a German metal table and bench (see *Furnished Dollhouses* for photographs of more pieces from a complete set), metal bucket, dishpan, pitcher, dishes and silverware (table and bench $150+, bucket, dishpan and pitcher $30 each).

The bedroom has been furnished with an assortment of off-white wood furniture as well as several metal pieces. A pink metal chair and matching rocker provide space for the jointed bisque little girl dolls to sit. The old wood lamp with a cloth shade ($75+), the pressed brass framed picture on the back wall ($100+), and the brass framed photograph on the dresser also add interest to the setting ($50). The dolls are each 4.75" tall and both have painted features and applied wigs ($100+ each).

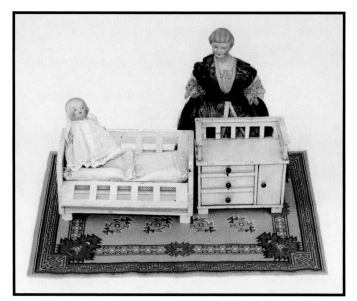

The nursery furniture includes a matching German wood crib and dresser. The sides of the crib fold down (set $75-100). The German all bisque baby is 3" tall ($50) while the German dollhouse grandmother is 7.75" high ($200).

The nursery furnishings also include a metal baby bath that probably came originally with a bucket hanging on the spigot. The metal washstand is from the bedroom. It has been repainted (bath $40-50, washstand $65+).

Small dollhouse size baby bathtubs were still being advertised by G. Sommers and Co. of St. Paul, Minnesota in 1929. The smallest version was 6.5" long by 6" high. Several small buggies were also pictured. *From the collection of Marge Meisinger.*

The Chicago Butler Bros. firm advertised dollhouse size metal washstands in their October 1929 catalog. The stands measured 6.5" high x 3.75" wide and came with a mirror, ewer, and basin. *From the collection of Marge Meisinger.*

Handmade wood dollhouse, perhaps from England, circa 1900. The trim on the house is made of walnut. The left side of the roof is hinged to provide storage. The sides of the house extend to the bottom, although the front and back do not. In this way an interesting base is provided. The house has been repainted ($800-900). 31" high (not including chimney) x 26" wide x 15" deep.

The inside of the handmade house has also been redecorated. The four rooms have been furnished as a kitchen, parlor, bathroom, and bedroom. The kitchen furnishings include an iron cook stove thought to have been made by J.& E. Stevens Co. of Cromwell, Connecticut. The parlor furnishings include an iron table and chair also made by the Stevens firm, circa 1880s, and a pressed tin parlor sofa and chair made by the George W. Brown Co. of Forestville, Connecticut, circa 1870s.

The bathroom is furnished with a German wood bathroom set sold by the New York firm of F.A.O. Schwarz. Several of the pieces carry their original stickers from the store. The bottom base of the pedestal sink has been replaced. The set includes a large storage piece with working drawers and mirror and a short table suitable for holding towels as well as the bathtub, sink, and toilet (set $250).

The house includes many old accessories. Included are ormolu pictures ($125+ each), mirror ($125), and wall clock ($150-175).

Several dollhouse dolls inhabit the large house. Included is a 5" all bisque jointed German girl marked "4527/4" on her back. She has glass eyes and a mohair wig ($100-125). She is getting ready to practice her violin ($150), which is an old German candy container.

The bedroom is furnished with a German wood desk and chair along with a German soft metal sewing basket ($75). On top of the desk are a vintage lamp ($95) and an inkwell set ($110).

The lady of the house is a German 7" tall dollhouse doll with painted features and a mohair wig. Beside her is an ormolu plant stand ($150 from the parlor) holding a brass framed picture ($50+). The metal German Marklin bed from the bedroom is also pictured ($250+). The doll has been redressed ($225+).

Austrian Bronze

Austrian Bronze (sometimes called Vienna Bronze) pieces are very much in demand for use as accessories in the older dollhouses. Although some of the potted flowers have been made more recently, the most desirable pieces are those produced from the late 1800s to the 1920s. These are usually marked "Austria." The metal items were made with "cold painting" meaning the pieces were not fired after the paint was applied. Pictured are several of the old desirable Austrian Bronze items. The sewing machine, cat, and stool were all made in one piece. The sewing machine is approximately 2.5" tall x 3" wide. It has no moving parts ($200). The animal sitting on the bottom of the machine and the other cat are separate pieces ($55+ each). *Photograph and accessories from the collection of Ruth Petros.*

This ormolu basket, trimmed with flowers, includes two Austrian Bronze flower pots and flowers mounted in special holders. The basket sits on a German marble topped table (basket and pots $250+). *Petros Collection.*

Several outdoor Austrian Bronze pieces are pictured in this outdoor setting. Most of these items are marked "Austria" on the bottom. The cactus plants range in size from 1" to 2" high. The Austrian Bronze tree is 4" tall. The bird is 1" wide x 1/2" high. All of these items were made in the early years of production (cactus $95-125 each, tree $150+, bird $55+). *Petros Collection.*

German Dollhouse Dolls

German dollhouse doll, circa 1910, featuring a very nice molded hair style with a bun on top. She has a bisque head, bisque lower arms and legs, and painted features. She is 6.25" tall and was very nicely redressed long ago in a fancy corset. Her current owner displays her in front of a full length mirror as if she is in the process of dressing for a fancy party ($200+). *Carey Collection.*

Early German dollhouse dolls with bisque heads, bisque lower arms and legs, and cloth bodies. They make very nice tenants for dollhouses from the late 1800s through 1920. The lady doll hair styles from the era feature buns (either on the top or at the back of the head) or applied wigs. Many of the faces of the masculine dolls are decorated with mustaches or beards in keeping with the styles of the day. These dolls are wearing their original commercially made clothing. Many dolls were sold nude and even though they were dressed at home soon after they were acquired, the outfits are not considered to be original clothing. These two dolls have painted features and molded hair and are each 6.25" tall ($200+ each.) *Photograph and dolls from the collection of Gail and Ray Carey.*

German dollhouse doll 6.25" tall with hair molded in a bun in the back. This doll was redressed many years ago in an old fashioned bathing suit. When her current owner moved to a warmer climate, she set up this beach scene (with a vintage postcard as background) and used the picture on her Christmas cards to send to friends along with her new address ($175+). *Carey Collection.*

German 7" dollhouse man wearing his original costume. His hat is on the chair beside him. He wears black bisque boots with tan paper tops and gold and red decorations on his suit. It is not known if he is dressed as a livery driver or in some kind of local costume ($200-225). *Carey Collection.*

1910s

N.D. Cass Co.

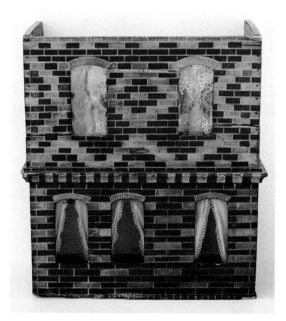

Unusual unidentified wood dollhouse with glass windows, circa 1915. The house has no roof or door and is open in the back. The brick design on its three sides is quite intricate and was made directly on the wood ($250+). 22.5" high x 20.5" wide x 11" deep.

The open back provides access to the house's three rooms. The house retains its original wall and floor papers. The upstairs wallpaper border pictures various toys of the period. The downstairs curtains are original while the ones upstairs have been replaced. The house has been furnished as a bathroom, dining room, and children's room. The bathroom furniture is German and includes a metal medicine cabinet on the wall.

Oak furniture manufactured by the N.D. Cass Co. of Athol, Massachusetts was used to furnish the dining room. The printing on the original box states that the set is No. 1075. The company was advertising doll furniture as early as 1910.

The Cass boxed dining room furniture included a dining room table, side table, breakfront, and four chairs. The chairs are easy to recognize because of the circle cut-out in the backs. The scale of the furniture is approximately 1.25" to one foot (boxed set $175+).

The children's room has been furnished with an oak set of small 1" to one foot scaled bedroom furniture, probably made in Germany, circa 1910-1915. It is known that the same company also made a matching dining room set. The doors and drawers are functional (set $175).

The dolls who inhabit the children's bedroom were also made in Germany. They have bisque heads, composition jointed bodies, painted features, and mohair wigs. They are both wearing their original clothing and the girl still carries her original doll. The boy is 4.75" tall and the girl measures 5.75". Several of their toys are pictured with them. Included is a metal train engine, a crocheted dog and a "Match-Box Sick Room" (dolls $125-150 each).

These small "Match-Box" creations make perfect toys for a dollhouse. This one is titled "Sick-Room." Many other designs were produced including a ski scene and a kitchen. Thought to have been made in Germany (MIB $40).

Moritz Gottschalk

Handmade wood dollhouse, circa 1910, that was made by a twelve year old boy for his younger sister. The house was constructed of old crates but it does have glass windows. It has been repainted ($250+). 39" high x 16.5" wide x 15" deep.

The front of the handmade house opens in two sections to reveal four large rooms, which include a bedroom, dining room, parlor, and kitchen. The room on the upper left includes the original wallpaper. The other rooms have been redecorated using older wallpapers. The house has been furnished mostly with German Gottschalk furniture from the period. The fireplaces in the parlor and dining room have been added. Most of the accessories in the house are old including two Gottschalk pictures and a mirror.

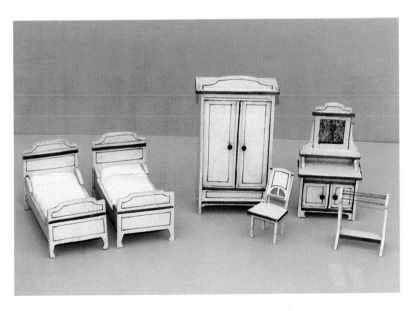

The bedroom furniture used in the house was pictured in the Gottschalk catalog for 1907 as documented in the *Moritz Gottschalk 1892-1931* book (see Bibliography). Other items also pictured in the catalog as part of the set include a night stand and a plant stand. The furniture is 1" to one foot in scale (set $350-400).

Gottschalk furniture used in the dining room and living room include a grandfather clock shown in the 1910 company catalog and chairs and a sofa that date from 1909. The plant stand is also a Gottschalk product. All of the furniture is 1" to one foot in scale. The redressed German 6.75" doll has a bisque head and lower limbs on a cloth body. He sports a handlebar mustache (doll $200, furniture $30-$75 each).

The dining room of the house includes a large Gottschalk breakfront from 1910 and a Gottschalk table and chairs. The German metal upright typewriter measures 1.5" wide x 1.75" deep and 1.25" tall. The crank on the side can be turned (breakfront $125+, typewriter $125+).

The house also includes a German baby in residence along with his walker, metal crib, and buggy. The all bisque, 2.75" tall baby has movable arms and stationary legs. He was advertised in the Butler Bros. catalog in 1929 complete with his wood walker. The metal crib on wheels is also a German product as is the soft metal buggy complete with an umbrella. The filigree pewter buggy measures 4.75" long. Similar buggies were advertised in the Butler Brothers catalog in 1914. The same model sold for several years (buggy $75+, crib $40-50, bisque doll in walker ($40-50).

The kitchen is furnished with a tin cookstove and metal shelf (not pictured), both made in Germany, as well as a wood table and chairs also from Germany. The blue metal dishes are like those sold by Tootsie Toy in the 1920s. A wood sink, bench, and metal icebox complete the furnishings. The old accessories include a granite dish pan, box of Rinso soap, metal carpet sweeper, and a set of metal glasses and matching pitcher. A 6" tall German dollhouse doll with painted features and an applied wig is in charge of the kitchen (metal shelf with accessories $75+, granite dishpan $35+, dishes $30, stove $65, sink $50+, doll $200+).

G. & J. Lines

This large house was produced by the English G.& J. Lines firm, circa 1900. The house is painted white with added gold trim. The lower story is papered with brick paper while the roof's paper represents shingles. It is missing one of its chimneys. The house was still being featured in the Lines catalog in 1909. A similar Lines house included curved style windows on the second and third floors and different trim above those windows (not enough examples to determine price). 52" high x 33.5" wide x 22" deep. *From the collection of Angel's Attic. Photographs by Jeff Carey.*

The inside of the early Lines house includes six rooms and three halls that feature staircases. The rooms of the house have been furnished as a kitchen, dining room, music room, parlor, and two bedrooms. *Angel's Attic Collection, Jeff Carey photograph.*

The kitchen is located in the lower left of the Lines house. A china head German doll has assumed the role of cook and a smaller china head little girl doll watches the activity. The wallpaper appears to be original to the house as are the kitchen dresser and fireplace. China plates are displayed over the fireplace and pewter plates spruce up the shelves in the corner. A German clothes basket is in the foreground (kitchen dresser $150+, clothes basket $35-50). *Angel's Attic Collection, Jeff Carey photograph.*

The dining room is located on the bottom right of the Lines house. It, too, features the original wallpaper and fireplace. The German furnishings include a marble top sideboard, oak chairs, and a grandfather clock, table, and cabinet in a mahogany finish. A German dinner gong is displayed on top of the fireplace and treenware dishes are featured on the table (gong $50+, treenware dishes $250+, marble top sideboard $125+). *Angel's Attic Collection, Jeff Carey photograph.*

The parlor is located on the second floor on the right. The room features its original wallpaper and fireplace. A unique brass mirror and fender decorate the fireplace. The room is furnished with a light colored German Biedermeier parlor set. An unusual corner cabinet hangs on the wall and an ormolu light fixture and a gold birdcage add interest to the room (birdcage $300+, rare blonde Biedermeier six piece parlor set $1,000+). *Angel's Attic Collection, Jeff Carey photograph.*

The music room (second story, left) also includes its original fireplace and what appears to be its original wallpaper. A filigree mirror as well as an unusual peacock fire screen decorate the fireplace. A three piece German parlor set and piano provide most of the furniture for the room. Accessories include a wall clock, pots of flowers, and several pictures (wall clock $175+, piano $125+). *Angel's Attic Collection, Jeff Carey photograph.*

G.& J. Lines English house, circa 1906. A similar house was featured in the Gamages London toy store catalog in that year. The house was painted white with gold trim and the roof was lithographed paper. The left chimney is a replacement ($1,200-1,500.) 26" high x 18.5" wide x 16" deep. *Private Collection.*

The inside of the house contains two large rooms. The downstairs has been fitted out as a Haberdasher's store while the upstairs serves as living quarters for the owner of the business. Dollhouse dolls of various types and sizes are featured in both rooms. A sewing machine and umbrella stand are some of the many accessories in the shop. The upstairs accessories include a variety of pictures, lamps, candlesticks, and vases. *Private Collection.*

Two 4.75" tall German Loofah trees with papier mâché bottoms, circa 1930s. The trees make interesting accessories in the yards of appropriate sized dollhouses. They were probably originally used in train and nativity displays ($35-50 pair). *Trees from the collection of Gail and Ray Carey. Photograph by Gail Carey.*

English Lines house No. 31, circa 1909-1910 (shown in catalog reproduction from that year). The house has brick paper on the sides and second story. The interesting window treatment and balcony add architectural details to the house ($1,200-1,500). 32" high x 24" wide x 17" deep. *Photographs and house from the collection of Patty Cooper.*

The inside of No. 31 contains four rooms with the original fireplaces. The wallpaper has been replaced. The rooms have been furnished as a living room, dining room, bedroom, and bathroom. The kitchen dresser and bathroom cabinet came with the house. Most of the house is furnished with German golden oak. The bathroom is also furnished with German pieces. *Cooper Collection.*

This German three piece upholstered parlor set could also be used to furnish a Lines house of the period. The scale for this furniture is a small 1" to one foot (set $75+). *Photograph by Suzanne Silverthorn.*

English G.& J. Lines house, circa 1915. A three-story version of this house is shown in Marion Osborne's photocopies of the 1915 Gamages catalog. The house has metal window frames and glass windows. The roof is lithographed paper and the house has two chimneys ($1,800+). 28" high x 26.5" wide x 18" deep. *Photograph and house from the collection of Patty Cooper.*

The inside of the 1915 Lines house contains four rooms plus two hallways. The house is furnished mostly with 1" to one foot scaled German red-stained furniture from the 1920s. The rooms include a dining room, living room, and two bedrooms. The inside of the house has probably been repapered. *Cooper Collection.*

This upholstered sofa, chair, piano, bench, and chest are from the German line of red-stained furniture and would also be appropriate pieces to use in furnishing this house (sofa and chair $65-75, piano and bench $65, chest $35). *Photograph by Suzanne Silverthorn.*

G.& J. Lines English Tudor house, circa 1931. This #38 styled house features metal window frames and glass panes. Unlike most of the Lines houses, this model includes a garage. The lower story is covered with brick paper while the rest of the house has been given a "stucco" look. Two chimneys, flower boxes. and "shrubs" on either side of the front door complete the "extra" touches ($900+). 26" high x 24" wide x 14" deep. *Photographs and house from the collection of Linda Boltrek.*

The inside of the Lines house has been furnished as a kitchen, combination living room-dining room, bedroom, and bathroom. Both German and English furniture have been used as furnishings. The dining room table and chairs and the living room wing chair and ottoman are thought to have been made by the English Tri-ang firm. A German Biedermeier sofa and soft metal piano are also used in the living room (wing chair and ottoman $100-125, piano and stool $150-195). *Boltrek Collection.*

The original Lines trademark is still on the house. It reads "G & J. L. L^td LONDON." Boltrek Collection.

Collection of baby buggies that would be suitable for use as accessories with dollhouses of this period. Included are a German soft metal buggy in the left back, a small metal model made in France in the middle back, and a nineteenth century buggy with original drapery in the left front. *Photograph and buggies from the collection of Linda Boltrek.*

Handmade Houses

Handmade house that has the look of the Schoenhut houses from the early 1920s, although this house appears to be earlier. The house originally could only be accessed from the open door and windows in the back. The front has been cut so that it could be removed and a door and window glass have been added to the back ($250+). 24" high x 15" wide x 15.5" deep.

With the front removed, the two rooms of the house can be nicely displayed. The house has been furnished with Star-American Toy Furniture, circa 1910-1917. This furniture is larger than 1" to one foot in scale. The dining room pieces are oak while the parlor furniture is finished in a walnut stain. The set of dining room furniture was advertised in the John Smyth catalog in 1917. The seven piece set sold for $1.25. The rooms have been redecorated using color copies of old wallpaper (unboxed Star furniture sets $100-150 each.)

The rooms of the handmade house are large enough to accommodate these two German Bonnet head dolls measuring 7" and 7.5" tall. The heads and lower arms and legs are made of white bisque while the bodies and upper limbs are cloth. Both dolls have been redressed. They fit nicely with the larger scale Star furniture ($150-175 each).

This 4.5" tall all bisque jointed doll plays with her toys in the upstairs room while the ladies chat. She has glass eyes and a mohair wig. She has been redressed. Her German dog is made of a celluloid type material (doll $100-125, dog $35+).

Star Novelty works of Cincinnati, Ohio made many different models of their large dollhouse furniture. The furniture was also labeled American Toy Furniture. This box is for a Parlor Set No. 60, which dates from around 1910.

Star furniture that came in the No. 60 box. Most of the oak furniture made by the firm has a rough feel, unlike the nicer Germen golden oak pieces. This parlor set includes a sofa, table, large mirror, two side chairs, and an arm chair. For more information and photographs of Star furniture please consult the earlier dollhouse books (boxed set $200).

Samples of the wallpaper used to paper the handmade house. Although the patterns look older, they came from the *Sears Roebuck & Co. Wall Paper* book from 1923. With the use of a color copier, old wallpaper samples can be duplicated to give an authentic look to a dollhouse that needs restoration.

Mason & Parker

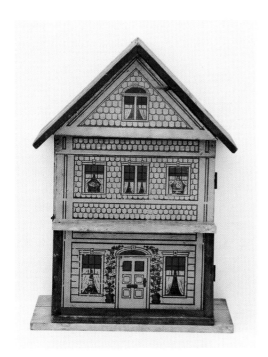

Lithographed wood house featured in the Winchendon, Massachusetts Mason & Parker Mfg. Co. catalog in 1914. The house came in four sizes, with heights of 13", 16", 20.5", and 22.5". This house is the smallest model. The house is missing its chimney ($500+). 13" high x 7.75" wide x 6.5" deep.

The inside of the Mason & Parker house contains two decorated rooms. Windows, wallpaper, and floor coverings have been lithographed on the walls and floors. The house has been furnished with the early Tootsietoy metal furniture, which is the right scale for the house. This early styled furniture was marketed by the Chicago based Dowst Brothers firm beginning in the early 1920s. The all bisque jointed little girl doll also dates from the 1920s (furniture $100, doll $40+).

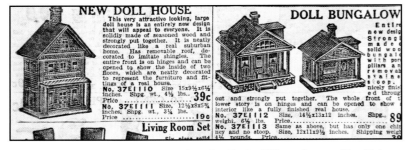

This same house was featured in an ad from the Charles Williams Stores in New York City circa 1914. The smaller house sold for only 19 cents. Two other houses featured in the Mason & Parker 1914 catalog were also sold by the Charles Williams Stores (see *Furnished Dollhouses* book for more information and photographs). They sold for 39 cents and 89 cents each. The copy for all the houses stated that they were new designs as did the advertising in the Mason & Parker catalog for 1914.

Other small furniture of the period could also be used to furnish the Mason & Parker house. This marked German wood table and four chairs is still glued to its original card. The furniture is approximately 1/2" to one foot in scale ($40+).

1920s

Gottschalk Red Roof

German Moritz Gottschalk "Red Roof" house. A similar house is pictured in their 1912 catalog as shown in the book *Moritz Gottschalk 1891-1931*. The book contains reprints of catalog illustrations from the photo archives of J. & M. Cieslik. The house in the catalog has different window and door treatments but otherwise is the same design, including the front and side porches. The gazebo is also thought to be a Gottschalk product although it did not come with the house ($4,500-5,000). 30" high x 27" wide x 18" deep. *Photographs and house from the collection of Ruth Petros.*

The inside of the large Gottschalk house has four rooms and an attic. The attic can be accessed through the small hinged door on the third floor. The wallpaper is original to the house. The downstairs hall includes a stairway and a door which opens to a toilet closet. The rest of the bathroom facilities are upstairs. The other two rooms have been furnished as a parlor and a kitchen. Small 1" to one foot scale German furniture and accessories have been used to furnish the house. *Petros Collection.*

The rare German figures sitting outside the house are made of a composition type material and have bobbing heads. They are approximately 4" tall in a sitting position ($150-200). *Petros Collection.*

Red Roof #5600 house pictured in the 1921 Gottschalk catalog according to the Moritz Gottschalk book. The three-story house has two bay windows, a second story balcony, and a hinged roof to provide access to the third story ($2,000-2,200). 21.5" high x 17.5" wide x 9.25" deep.

The front of the house opens to provide access to the lower four rooms and the hinged roof lifts to reveal the third floor bedroom and bathroom. All of the wall and floor coverings are original. Most of the furniture is also original to the house. The front hall contains a stairway and a built-in toilet in the closet.

A 4.75" German dollhouse doll sits on the original sofa. The doll has a bisque head, hands and feet, and a cloth body. He is wearing his original clothing. The Gottschalk 3/4" to one foot pressed cardboard furniture used to furnish the parlor is original to the house. Included are a sofa, desk, and three chairs ($15-40 each piece, doll $125+).

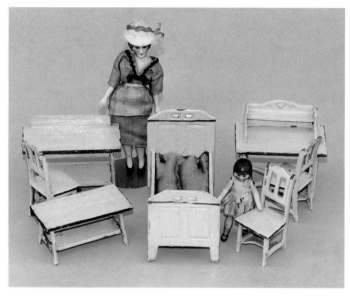

These pieces of 3/4" to one foot pressed cardboard furniture are also original to the house. Included are a bed, chairs, desks, and a low table. Pictured with the furniture are two German dollhouse dolls in their original clothing. The woman is 4.75" tall and the little girl is 3" tall. Both have molded hair and painted features (furniture $15-40 each, girl $50+, woman $100-125).

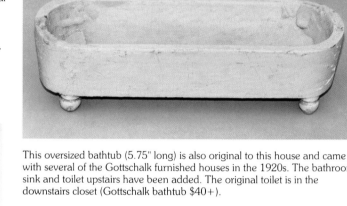

This oversized bathtub (5.75" long) is also original to this house and came with several of the Gottschalk furnished houses in the 1920s. The bathroom sink and toilet upstairs have been added. The original toilet is in the downstairs closet (Gottschalk bathtub $40+).

Gottschalk furniture used in the kitchen includes only the table and chairs. The German wood sink and tin cooking stove have been added. The 4.75" tall German maid carries a metal pan tied to her arm (original maid $125+, stove $50+, table and chairs $60 set, sink $40).

Besides original furniture, the house also includes two original pictures and a shelf. The dishes have been added. Surprisingly, the pictures are identical, showing the same scene. All three items were made of pressed cardboard by the Moritz Gottschalk firm ($25-40 each).

Gottschalk Red Roof two-room house, circa 1921. A similar house from the 1921 catalog is pictured in the Moritz Gottschalk book. The house has a gabled dormer and a porch across the front ($1,000-1,200). 15" high x 19.5" wide x 11" deep. *Photographs and house from the collection of Linda Boltrek.*

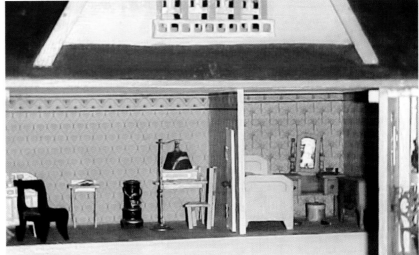

The inside of the two-room house includes Gottschalk furniture as well as other German pieces, including a kerosene metal stove. The wallpaper appears to be original. *Boltrek Collection.*

The bottom of the house is stamped "Made in Germany" and the number 5993 is written on the original Lord & Taylor sticker tag along with the price of $10.95. *Boltrek Collection.*

Although the kerosene stove was used in the furnishings of this house, a fireplace would also have been appropriate in the proper size. Pictured are a variety of metal fireplaces and stoves ranging in size from 2.5" high to 4" high and 2.5" to 6.3" wide. Both English and German models are shown. The brown cast iron fireplace was sold by the English Tri-ang firm, and the black fireplace is also English. The gray fireplace on the left was once in the Vivian Green collection. The other fireplaces and stoves are thought to be German in origin. *Boltrek Collection.*

This Gottschalk house with a garage, #6759, is very similar to one pictured in the *Moritz Gottschalk 1892-1931* book in the catalog reprint for 1925. The catalog picture shows the house with different mullions in the windows and a small porch overhang with plain pillars. Because not very many of the Gottschalk houses included garages, this house is especially desirable. The house also includes a gable roof, an upstairs side porch, and opening garage doors ($1,500+). 15" high x 16.5" wide x 10" deep. *Photographs and house from the collection of Ruth Petros.*

The inside of the house can be accessed through a front opening and a hinged roof. It includes three rooms with a stairway in the downstairs. The house has been furnished with some Gottschalk pieces as well as other German furniture. *Petros Collection.*

The German pressed cardboard furniture on the upstairs porch was advertised in the Butler Brothers Chicago catalog in 1929. The set included a table and four chairs (table 3.25" across, chairs approximately 3" tall). The set also included three bisque dolls and a cardboard plate. The furniture has been identified by Swantje Kohler as "Korbi," which was made by Karl Schreifer in Germany. *From the collection of Marge Meisinger. Photograph by Suzanne Silverthorn.*

A set of German "Korbi" pressed cardboard furniture similar to that pictured in the Butler Bros. ad and like that used on the upstairs porch of the Gottschalk house with a garage. This set includes the "hard to find" large rocking chair (set $150, including rocker). *Petros Collection.*

German Gottschalk "Red Roof" garden house, circa 1927. A similar house was pictured in the company's catalog that year. Although some of the side porch turnings are missing, the original catalog picture confirms that no turnings were ever placed on the porch next to the front of the house ($2,000). 21" high x 20.5" wide X 10.5" deep. *Photographs and house from the collection of Ruth Petros.*

The front of the "garden house" pulls down to reveal a garden. The original house came with a small fence, flowers, shrubs, and lawn furniture. The fence, shrubs, flowers, trees, fountain, and other accessories in this garden have been added and/or replaced. *Petros Collection.*

The inside of the house is revealed when the garden is in place. It includes two large rooms and two smaller rooms that could be considered halls. Another room can be accessed by lifting the hinged roof. The downstairs hall contains a stairway and closet housing a toilet. The house has been furnished with mostly Gottschalk pressed cardboard furniture in 1/2" to one inch scale. *Petros Collection.*

The furnishings in the third floor include a German kerosene heater as well as pressed cardboard Gottschalk furniture. *Petros Collection.*

German Gottschalk red roof "stucco" house, circa 1930. This house is pictured in the Moritz Gottschalk book in the catalog reprints for 1930. Interest is added to this house by including both a side porch and a garage. The house is missing its chimney ($2,500-3,000). 21" high x 35" wide x 13" deep. *Photographs and house from the collection of Dollhouse and Miniature Museum of Cape May.*

The inside of the "stucco" house includes four large rooms and two halls, all with original wallpapers. The rooms have been furnished as a kitchen, sitting room, and two bedrooms. Four nice German dollhouse dolls live in the house. The male doll has a molded hat ($250+), the maid, grandmother, and lady dolls are all approximately 5" tall ($125-150 each). *Dollhouse and Miniature Museum of Cape May.*

The downstairs hall also includes a closet containing a toilet, as did many of the Red Roof Gottschalk houses. Most of the house has been furnished with German furniture and accessories, including the desk at the top of the stairs. This wood furniture is 3/4" to one foot in scale. *Dollhouse and Miniature Museum of Cape May.*

Close-up of the sitting room furnished with German furniture and two German dollhouse dolls. *Dollhouse and Miniature Museum of Cape May.*

Gottschalk house with an unusual green roof that appears in the Gottschalk catalog of 1930 according to the reprints in the Moritz Gottschalk book. The house includes an enclosed side porch as well as a decorative over hang at the front door. The chimney has been replaced ($600-800). 12.5" high (excluding chimney) x 21.5" wide x 9.5" deep. *Photographs and house from the collection of Marianne Price.*

The front of the green roof Gottschalk house opens in two sections to reveal the downstairs rooms. The second floor room can be accessed through its hinged opening. The downstairs has been furnished as a living room and a kitchen. Newer dressed mice inhabit the house. The living room is furnished with a German Biedermeier sofa and chair and an English Taylor & Barrett fireplace. The kitchen pieces include a German tin stove and German wood table, chairs, and sink (Stove $50). *Price Collection.*

The small upstairs bedroom is furnished with a painted German wood night stand and vanity, along with a German soft metal bed. *Price Collection.*

The painted German furniture used in the house is in a small 3/4" to one foot scale. The doors are functional (sink $40, others $75 set). *Price Collection.*

This "castle" type German Red Roof Gottschalk house appears in the Gottschalk catalog in 1930, according to the reprints in the Moritz Gottschalk book. The house has been given a stucco look along with a tower. The curved openings, balcony, and over-the-door trim give the house a "Spanish" look. The bottom of the house is stamped "Made in Germany" ($1,500-1,800). 18" high x 22" wide by 14" deep. *Photographs and house from the collection of Ruth Petros.*

The inside of the house contains four rooms plus a small attic "tower" space that can be used for storage. The stairway room includes a toilet closet under the stairs. The house retains its original wall and floor coverings. The house has been furnished with an assortment of German furniture in a 3/4" to one foot scale. *Petros Collection.*

The upstairs bedroom features two bisque dolls that were in the house when it came to the present owner. The furniture includes a German bed, dresser, and small wardrobe. A Gottschalk picture hangs on the wall. An interesting German tin "penny" toy is also located in the bedroom. It is a highchair that folds down to a small table and chair. These "penny" toys were made in the early 1900s in a 1/2" to one inch scale. Because they are small and were easily broken, they are hard to find in excellent condition ($200-300 each). *Petros Collection.*

The dining room furnishings include an interesting Gottschalk pressed cardboard fireplace and a German three piece wood table, cabinet, and mirror. The furniture is decorated with paper trim that has been designed to look like metal. *Petros Collection.*

Frier Steel

Advertisement for the COZYTOWN cottage made by the Frier Steel Company located in St. Louis, Missouri. According to the ad from 1928 the house was priced at $9.00.

This advertisement from the 1929 Butler Brothers Chicago catalog pictured the iron Kilgore furniture in a variety of sets. These included a Sally Ann Household package featuring a sweeper, washer (with wringer), stove, and ladder. The nursery set and playground sets are also shown. A larger buggy (5" x 5.75") is also included. *From the collection of Marge Meisinger.*

Frier Steel Cozytown Cottage as pictured in the 1928 advertisement ($125+ in this condition). The house is of all-steel construction and was one of three different models offered by the company (see *Furnished Dollhouses* for photographs of the other two models). 12" high x 14" wide x 10" deep.

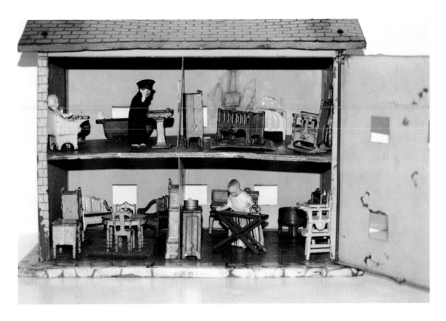

The inside of the Cozytown Cottage contains four rooms that have been furnished with iron "Kilgore" furniture along with a few pieces of metal Tootsietoy furniture in the living room. The rooms have been furnished as a kitchen, living room-dining room combination, bathroom, and bedroom-nursery.

Tri-ang

English Triangtois Cottage No. DH/B. This small house was advertised by the firm in 1921. The house was papered in brick paper on the first story and finished with a stucco look on the second floor ($600-700). 21.5" high x 14" wide x 7.5" deep. *From the collection of Gail and Ray Carey. Photographs by Gail Carey.*

The inside of the cottage contains two rooms furnished as a parlor and a bedroom. The furniture was made in Germany and is in a small 1" to one foot scale. The wallpapers and floor coverings appear to be original. *Carey Collection.*

The parlor furnishings feature a German set which includes a sofa (6" wide x 3.75" high), three chairs, glass fronted cabinet, and marble topped piece with a mirror (six pieces $250+). Two German dollhouse dolls are also pictured. They are all original. The man is 5.25" tall and the maid is 4.75" in height ($125 each). *Carey Collection.*

Tri-ang Tudor style house #62 featuring two gables and a garage. This style of house in various models was marketed by the English Tri-ang firm from the 1930s until the 1950s. The house has had some repainting ($400-500). 16.5" high x 26.5" wide x 10.75" deep.

The inside of the Tri-ang Tudor house contains four rooms. They have been furnished as a dining room, kitchen, bedroom, and a bathroom. The house has been repapered. The dining room is furnished with English Tudor wood furniture that was made by A. Barton and Co. from the late 1940s until the 1970s. The cast metal bathroom pieces were marketed under the "Fairylite" trade name by Graham Bros. of London shortly after World War II.

"My Dolly's Kitchen Series" was made of tin by Brimtoy in Great Britain, circa 1950s. Besides the stove, sink, cabinet, and refrigerator pictured, a washing machine was also a part of the set. The doors are functional. They are 3/4" to one foot in scale (MIB set $200+).

The chair, wardrobe, table, and lamp in the bedroom are thought to have been made by the English Pit-a-Pat firm, circa 1930s. The dollhouse doll has metal feet, a mohair wig, and is 3.5" tall.

Tynietoy

Tynietoy New England Town House #977. The Tynietoy houses and furniture were made and sold by the Toy Furniture shop in Providence, Rhode Island. The business partners were Marion I. Perkins and Amey Vernon. The products were on the market for several decades from the 1920s until the 1940s. This house was made in a Georgian style, painted white with green shutters. The front of the house can be removed for easy access to the rooms ($7,000). The main body of the house measures 29.5" high (not including chimney), 36" wide x 16.5" deep. The kitchen wing is 19.5" high x 11.5" wide x 10.75" deep. *Photographs and house from the collection of Ruth Petros.*

The inside of the Tynietoy house includes six rooms, two halls, and a three-room attic (accessed by lifting the hinged roof). The house has been furnished as a kitchen, dining room, living room, nursery, and two bedrooms, using mostly Tynietoy furniture. The attic rooms include another bedroom, playroom, and a storage area. *Petros Collection.*

Ask Santy to bring your doll house these Tynietoys from the Toy Furniture Shop. Andirons ($1.50) for the fireplace ($1.65) an enchanting replica of an 18th Century wing chair ($2.35) a hand-woven rug ($0.35) old-time candlesticks in silver or brass ($0.75) a Terry clock with hand-painted picture ($1.00). Entire set, $8.25.

Tynietoy advertisement from *Child Life* magazine for December 1930. The pictured wing chair that was priced at $2.25 now sells for $250-400 or more. The fireplace cost $1.65 and the Terry clock sold for $1.00.

The kitchen furniture includes a Tynietoy breakfast nook, Tynietoy cabinet, Strombecker sink, and German 1920s dollhouse maid. The upstairs nursery features the Tynietoy nursery set, consisting of crib, high chair, dresser, screen, table, and chairs (breakfast nook $400+). *Petros Collection.*

The Tynietoy bed in the bedroom next to the nursery was called a "Four-poster" in the Tynietoy catalog. It was priced at $4.75 (current price $200+). Originally the complete bedroom came with eleven pieces priced at $16.25. Included were a bureau, chair, washstand, pitcher and bowl, cradle, dressing table glass, stool, warming pan, rug, and pillow. The dining room is furnished with Tynietoy Sheraton pieces as well as a Tynietoy highboy. *Petros Collection.*

The front cover of an early Tynietoy catalog issued by the Toy Furniture Shop of Providence, Rhode Island, circa late 1920s (original catalog $75-100+). *Catalog from the collection of Leslie and Joanne Payne. Photographs by Suzanne Silverthorn.*

The Tynietoy catalog, issued by the Toy Furniture Shop of Providence, Rhode Island, circa late 1920s, included thirty-two pages of pictures and prices for both the furniture and houses. Pictured is a popular painted bedroom set ($9.00 set) as well as plainer (and cheaper) furniture to be used in a maid's bedroom. This unit was priced for $5.00. Most of the Tynietoy furniture was marked with their trademark of a two-story house with a pine tree on the left and a ladder back chair on the right. *Payne Collection.*

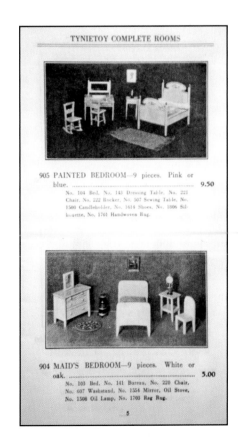

The largest of the Tynietoy dollhouses was the #975 Colonial Mansion. The house included nine rooms, three halls, and a pantry. In this catalog it was priced at $170 unfurnished and $261 furnished. Apparently the garden was also included. In 1930 the cost was $300 unfurnished and $460 furnished. It was 2 feet 8" high x 6 feet 2" wide x 1 foot 5.5" deep. *Payne Collection.*

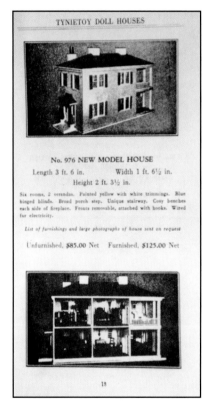

The New Model House #976 was a smaller Tynietoy house, measuring 2 feet 3.5" high x 3 feet 6" wide x 1 foot 6.5" deep. This house had six rooms and two porches. Like most of the Tynietoy homes, the front was removable. It was priced at $85 unfurnished and $125 furnished in the Tynietoy catalog. *Payne Collection.*

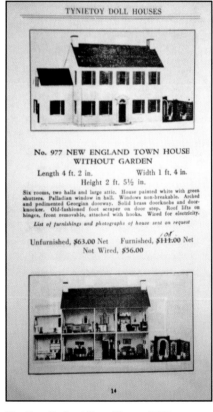

The New England Town House #977 was similar to the large Mansion house but it included only six rooms, two halls, and an attic. It measured 2 feet 5.5" tall x 4 feet 2" wide x 1 foot 4" deep. This house was priced at $63 unfurnished and $108 furnished. If sold without electricity, it cost only $56. *Payne Collection.*

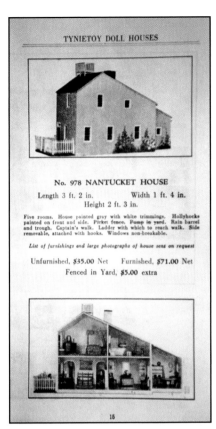

The Nantucket House #978 was a much cheaper Tynietoy house costing $35 unfurnished and $71 furnished. A fenced yard could be purchased for $5 extra. This house had five rooms and the outside was decorated with hollyhocks painted on its front and side. The side of the house was removable. A captain's walk on the roof and a ladder to reach it also came with the house. The house measured 2 feet 3" high x 3 feet 2" wide x 1 foot 4" deep. *Payne Collection*.

The four-room Village House #979 was the fifth house available from Tynietoy. The house sold for $18 unfurnished and $34 furnished. The side of the house was removable. The house measured 2 feet 1" high x 2 feet 4" wide x 1 foot 2" deep. *Payne Collection*.

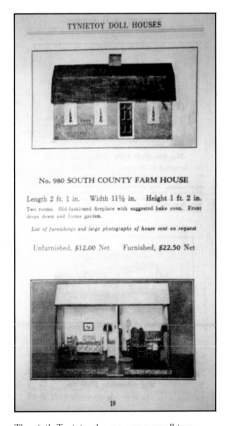

The sixth Tynietoy house was a small two-room house called the South Country House #980. It sold for $12 unfurnished and $22.50 furnished. The front was removable. It measured 1 foot 2" high x 2 foot 1" wide and 11.5" deep. For photographs of many of the Tynietoy houses see the earlier dollhouse books by the author. *Payne Collection*.

Tynietoy advertisement from *Child Life* magazine for December 1926. It pictured furniture for a music room and the Fourposter bedroom. The Wingchair was priced at $1.75, the piano (with music box) was $8.00, and the Sheraton Sofa cost $2.00.

Tynietoy ad which appeared in *Child Life* magazine for December 1929. It lists the prices of the six unfurnished Tynietoy houses at $250, $125, $85, $55, $30, and $17.50 (from largest to smallest). In an ad from 1930 the prices were $300, $125, $115, $60, $31, and $17.50. In both ads the Colonial Mansion included a garden, running water and electricity.

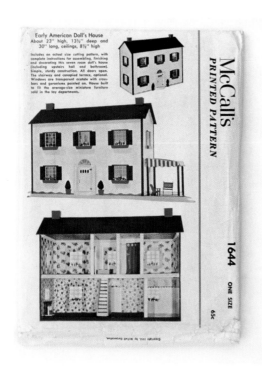

For those collectors unable to find or afford a real Tynietoy house, several dollhouse patterns have been made to allow collectors to build houses that would accommodate Tynietoy furniture. This #1644 McCalls pattern carries a 1951 copyright from McCall Corp. The "Early American Doll's House" provides room for a living room, dining room, kitchen, bedroom, hall, bathroom, and nursery. The finished house measures 23" high x 30" wide x 13.5" deep. The ceilings are 8.5" high.

Wagner

German dollhouse thought to be from D.H. Wagner & Sohn, circa late 1920s. The house has an interesting tower with bay windows on the front. The casement windows open and are made of metal. The roof has a mottled, stenciled pattern meant to look like tile and the walls are decorated in the same way to give the impression of brick. The Wagner houses are usually finished in this manner ($800-1,000). 17.5" high x 25" wide x 11" deep. *Photographs and house from the collection of Linda Boltrek.*

The inside of the house contains four rooms plus the entry. Most of the furnishings are in 1/2" to 3/4" to one foot scale. Soft metal German pieces add interest to the house. The bisque doll is also from Germany. *Boltrek Collection.*

An assortment of soft metal German furniture and accessories, some of which have been used in the Wagner house. Included are a screen ($100+), clock ($50+), plant stand ($100), and an umbrella stand ($75+). Also pictured are a birdcage, chair, table, and coat rack. *Boltrek Collection.*

Unknown German Houses

Unknown house, probably of German origin, circa 1920s. The wood house is colorfully decorated with flowers, shutters, flower boxes, a porch railing, and an unusual door treatment. A dormer window adds interest to the roof ($500-700). 18" high x 21" wide x 13" deep. *Photographs and house from the collection of Linda Boltrek.*

The inside of the house includes two rooms. The house has been furnished as a bedroom and sitting room. Most of the furniture and accessories are German in a 1/2" to 3/4" to one foot scale. *Boltrek Collection.*

The German sofa, four chairs, and table used to furnish the sitting room are in a 1/2" to 3/4" to one foot scale (set $175). *Boltrek Collection.*

This assortment of small bisque and china dolls ranges in size from 2" to 6" tall. All of them could be used as dollhouse dolls in the appropriate size houses. The two early china head dolls (standing on the round platform) are especially desirable. They both date from the nineteenth century and because of their small size (2.5" and 4") and unique hair styles, they would make wonderful inhabitants for old dollhouses. The 4.5" tall German bisque chauffeur on the right is also extra special. He is all original with his glasses pulled up to the top of his head. He has glass eyes. The all bisque doll with glass eyes and a wig on the left, the German bisque 3" doll in her original celluloid box, and the baby dolls in their fancy dresses would all add interest to dollhouses of the past. *Boltrek Collection.*

This house was probably handmade in Germany, circa 1920s. The house is decorated in a rough stucco finish with dark wood trim. The roof is "shingled" in dark green. It includes a yard platform with a fence ($400-600). 24.75" high x 24.5" wide x 24.5" deep. *Photographs and house from the collection of Bonnie Benson Hanson.*

The inside of the house includes five rooms that have been furnished as a living room, bedroom, bathroom, and downstairs and upstairs halls. The house includes electric lights with a panel on the back of the house that could be used to turn on the lights in each room. It has been furnished mostly with German furniture. Hanson Collection.

German furniture in 3/4" to one foot scale used in the house. The black stained furniture is marked "Germany" in white script-style printing. The soft metal clock is also German ($15-50 each piece). *Hanson Collection.*

The downstairs hall shows the interesting heavy lock on the front door as well as the stairway and electric light. Hanson Collection.

1930s

Converse

"Stucco" house made by the Morton E. Converse firm, located in Winchendon, Massachusetts. The house was advertised in the Montgomery Ward Spring and Summer catalog in 1931 priced at $2.69. The Converse dollhouse furniture was also pictured, priced at 89 cents a room. The house was 10" high x 13.75" wide x 11.75" deep (see *Furnished Dollhouses* for a photograph of a similar house). The catalog states that the house had wallpapered walls. Other Converse advertisements of the time stated that four different "stucco" houses were available. *From the collection of Marge Meisinger. Photograph by Suzanne Silverthorn.*

The largest model of the Converse stucco line of dollhouses includes six rooms. This house has two large dormer windows on the gable roof and interesting porch steps on the front and side of the house. These houses are easy to recognize because of their shutters, which are decorated with round holes ($500-600). *Photographs and house courtesy of Shirley C. Parks, Curator of Winchendon Historical Society, Home of Toy Museum of Converse and Mason & Parker Toys.*

The inside of the six-room Converse house is partly furnished with Converse "Realy Truly" furniture (kitchen and dining room). *Parks Collection.*

The back of the roof of the "Stucco" house lifts up to allow access to the six rooms inside. The house also contains a small side porch and steps. It is not known if the windows originally had cardboard mullions as did those of the smaller houses. *Parks Collection.*

This Converse "Stucco" house, circa early 1930s, contains only two rooms. It includes a front porch with posts, a railing, and the familiar shutters decorated with round holes. This house originally had cardboard mullions in the windows ($400+). 15.5" high x 22" wide x 17.5" deep.

The inside of the house retains its original paper doily curtains. These larger houses appear never to have had wallpaper on the walls. The two rooms have been furnished in a large 1" scale furniture which was sold by leading department stores circa late 1920s-early 1930s.

The living room pieces include a piano and bench, settee, drop front desk, chair, and planter. All of the doors and drawers are functional in this furniture. The only markings on the pieces are the names of the stores that sold the furniture. They include White House (San Francisco), F.A.O. Schwarz, and Marshall Field. Most of the furniture contains little finish although some pieces were varnished or painted (piano $40-50, desk $35-45, settee $35+, chair $15-20, plant stand $15-20).

The bedroom includes a poster bed, night stand, vanity and bench, rocker, cradle, and clothes rack. This line of furniture looks very much like the design used for the small 1" to one foot 1928 Schoenhut furniture. It may be that this furniture was produced in Germany and sold only to "high-end" stores in the U.S.A. If the furniture has not been painted, the small brads holding the furniture together can be seen (set of bed, night stand, vanity, bench, rocker $125, cradle $30, clothes rack $25).

The dining room serving cart was also made by the same unknown firm. Dolls in the house include a 6" German grandmother nicely redressed. She has molded hair, painted features, bisque limbs, and cloth body. The 4" jointed bisque girl has molded hair with hair bows, painted features, and is wearing a molded sun suit. The all bisque baby in the cradle has molded hair and features and jointed arms and legs. He has been redressed (cart $40-50, grandmother $200, girl $75).

These living room and dining room pieces were also made by the same unknown company. The doors and drawers function on the cabinet. Most of these pieces have an F.A.O. Schwarz sticker on the bottom (cabinet $75+, chairs $15-20 each, sofa $45-50, living room chair $35-45). *Photograph and furniture from the collection of Evangeline Steinmeier.*

This living room chair came with a matching sofa like the one already pictured. Both pieces were a natural color and had holes in their seats, perhaps to be used for upholstery (chair $35+). *Photograph and chair from the collection of Patty Cooper.*

Library table matching the other unknown furniture used to furnish the Converse house ($35-45). *Photograph and furniture from the collection of Gail and Ray Carey.*

Assortment of furniture thought to have been made by the same maker that supplied furniture to large department stores. This table looks very different from the plainer pieces in the line but it has been found several times accompanied by these chairs that are certainly part of the unknown F.A.O. Schwarz furniture (larger pieces $45-55 each). *Photograph and furniture from the collection of Patty Cooper.*

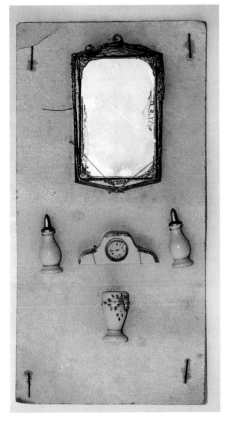

The early 1" to one foot scaled Dolly Dear Accessories (known then as R.T. Kirkland Co.) would work nicely with the larger houses and furniture from the 1930s. This carded set includes a mirror, candlesticks, clock, and vase (set on card $75).

Although this German Caco doll would not be big enough to live in the larger Converse houses of the 1930s, she would be the right size to accompany Converse "Really Truly" furniture of the era. This MIB Nursery set includes a nurse, baby, and oversized accessories. Box size 7" x 9" (MIB set $85+). *Photograph and set from the collection of Patty Cooper.*

Macris

Advertisement for a Dolly Ann dollhouse made by the Macris Company of Toledo, Ohio. It appeared in *Child Life* magazine for December 1930.

Macris Dolly Ann house advertised in *Child Life* magazine in 1930. The house sold for $12. It was made of composition board with a wood frame. The house had steel window frames with clear non shatter glass-like material used for the windows ($250+). 17.75" high x 18.5" wide x 14.25" deep. *Photographs and house from the collection of Ruth Petros.*

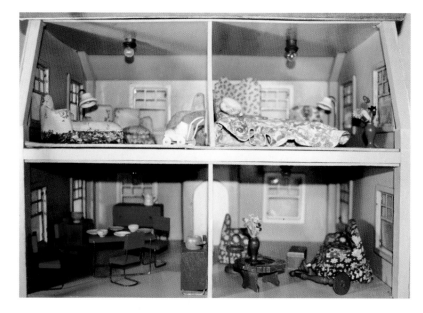

The inside of the Dolly Ann house includes four rooms that could be accessed by opening two hinged back sections. The house was electrified and could be plugged into a wall outlet. It has been furnished with mostly upholstered furniture from the 1930s and 1940s. The kitchen and dining room pieces in the downstairs are Miniaform, circa 1938. *Petros Collection.*

Menasha

These plans for a plywood dollhouse were featured in *Woman's Day* magazine in September 1945. The plans came in a booklet that could be ordered from the magazine. The house was designed by Cameron Clark. *From the collection of Marian Schmuhl.*

The inside of the *Woman's Day* dollhouse included a living room, dining room, kitchen (behind the dining room) in the lower story, and two bedrooms and a bathroom on the second floor. The house was supposed to have a garden area outside of the front door. *From the collection of Marian Schmuhl.*

This plywood house was made in the 1940s using the *Woman's Day* dollhouse pattern. It has been furnished mostly with the large scale Menasha furniture. This furniture was produced by the Menasha Woodenware Corporation, located in Menasha, Wisconsin, circa 1934. The ceramic bathroom was made in Japan at a later date. Nancy Ann Storybook bisque dolls from the early to mid 1940s live in the house. The house was redecorated in the 1960s (not original $300+). 28" high (not including chimney) x 36" wide x 22" deep.

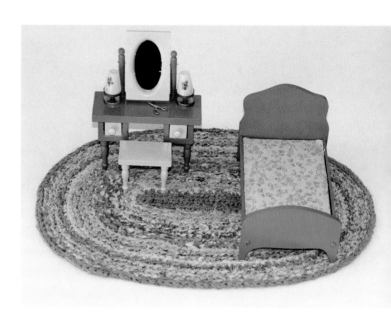

The Menasha Woodenware large scale bedroom furniture, along with two German rocking chairs, has been used to furnish the upstairs bedroom on the right. The bed is 7.5" long. Other Menasha bedroom pieces, including a night stand, may have also been produced. It is known that a rocking chair was made using the same type legs as those on the dining room chairs (Menasha $50 each).

The Menasha "Tyke Toys" large scale living room furniture included a sofa (6.75" long x 4" high), two chairs, and a floor lamp (repainted lampshade). A library table, end table, and perhaps a radio may also have been produced ($25-45 each piece).

The Menasha dining room pieces include a table, chairs, and sideboard. The chairs are 5" tall. The drawers are functional. The serving cart in the dining room was made in Germany and is not part of this set. A redressed bisque Nancy Ann Storybook doll is also pictured (set $100-125).

These Menasha Woodenware large scale pieces have been used to furnish the kitchen. Included are a sink, stove, cabinet, table and chairs. The oven door on the stove has been replaced (table and chairs $50-75, other items $50 each).

Two of the bisque Nancy Ann Storybook dolls who live in the *Woman's Day* house. The 5.5" girl dates from the mid-1940s and has jointed arms and stiff legs. She has been redressed ($10-15). The 4" baby has the "star" hands and is wearing his original clothing except for his jacket ($100+). The wood baby cradle is stamped "Germany" and has its original fittings.

Unidentified painted blue furniture with hand painted trim in a 1.25" to one foot scale has been used in two rooms of the house. This dining room sideboard is pictured against the back wall of the living room. The complete dining room set is shown in the Samm Burnham house in the 1890 section. The drawers and doors are functional. The maker of the furniture is unknown (chair $8-10, sideboard $35).

The Nancy Ann Storybook bisque Hush-a-Bye Baby doll is pictured with a metal buggy, circa mid to late 1930s, and a highchair, circa 1933. The high chair is made of wood except for a metal tray and footrest (baby [star hands, original clothes except for jacket] $100, buggy $35, high chair $20+).

Blue painted bedroom furniture matching the sideboard. The bed is 6.5" long. This furniture is used in one of the upstairs bedrooms (bed and dresser $35 each).

The Montgomery Ward Christmas catalog for 1933 advertised a three piece wood set that included a buggy, shoofly duck, and a high chair like the one used in the *Woman's Day* dollhouse. Two small bisque dolls also came with the package. The price in the Depression year of 1933 was only 49 cents.

Another example of the *Woman's Day* dollhouse from 1945. Although this looks like the side of the house, it contains the only door as well as several windows. The opening at the top matches the one on the other side so the house could be carried more easily. *Photograph and house from the collection of Marguerite Sweeney.*

Although this side of the house appears to be the front, there is no door. The roof on this house has the appearance of real shingles while the other example, shown earlier, featured a wood roof with etched lines drawn in a shingle pattern. *Sweeney Collection.*

The inside of this house includes "closets," a stairway, and what appears to be the original decoration, including curtains. *Sweeney Collection.*

The original handmade furniture accompanies this *Woman's Day* house. Most of it was made using the instructions published in the magazine's September 1945 issue. The kitchen stove-sink-cabinet was to be made from one block of wood with doors drawn on and outlined in red. The drawer and door pulls were to be made of tacks. The faucet is a bent nail. The pieces pictured here are a little different than those shown in the magazine, but have the same basic look. This refrigerator has a more rounded shape while the magazine example was straight edged. *Sweeney Collection*.

The bedroom furniture uses the same red and white theme as that shown in *Woman's Day* and the bed, dressing table, and stool (made from a spool) are very much like the magazine pieces. The bedroom chair supplied by the publication was a "slipper" design while this one is a chaise lounge. The bedroom curtains match the furniture. *Sweeney Collection*.

The nursery furniture in this house is similar to the pieces pictured in the magazine but instead of using a salt box for the cradle, this one is made of wood. The chest in the magazine was made from match boxes and the playpen was also made of cardboard. The "handy man" who made this nursery set used wood but still followed the "look" of the magazine pieces. *Sweeney Collection*.

The "Woman's Day" dining room furniture was made of plywood and included a table, four chairs, and a corner cabinet. This set also appears to be made from plywood but a server and a chest also are included. *Sweeney Collection*.

Miniaform

Rich Toys produced several Art Deco houses during their years in business. Although this house is not marked, it is similar to other Deco houses known to have been made by Rich Toy Co. of Clinton, Iowa ($350-400). 12" tall x 16.1" wide x 8.75" deep. *Photographs and house from the collection of George Mundorf.*

The inside of the house has been furnished with Miniaform 3/4" to one foot scale wood and wire furniture, circa 1939. *Mundorf Collection.*

Four boxes of Miniaform Art Deco furniture, circa 1939. The furniture was made by the Hugh Specialty Company of Chicago. Shown are kitchen, bedroom, dining room, and living room sets. Each box contains six pieces of the unique furniture ($125+ each boxed set). *Mundorf Collection.*

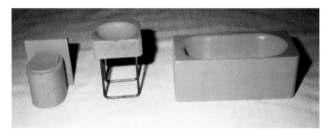

Bathroom set of wood and wire furniture by an unknown maker. It is known that a Miniaform bathroom was made; perhaps these are pieces from that set ($50+ set). *Photograph and set from the collection of Evangeline Steinmeier.*

Pit-a-Pat

"The Grange," an English house made by Amersham Works, Ltd. Although the metal diamond-paned windows are shown in a catalog of 1938, this house is probably later as it has a transfer Amersham label on the base. The Tudor house has a typical Amersham roof made with overlapping wood strips. This house is especially nice because it includes a garage ($500-600). 21" high x 34" wide x 12" deep. *Private Collection.*

The inside of the Amersham house has six rooms furnished with Pit-a-Pat English furniture. The rooms include a living room, dining room, kitchen, bedroom, music room, and bathroom. The Pit-a-Pat furniture was made by E. Lehman & Co. of London from 1932 until World War II. Although the furniture was listed briefly in the late 1940s, at that time the company was mostly involved in making games. *Private Collection.*

English Pit-a-Pat furniture used in the dining room and music rooms. The books were also Pit-a-Pat but the bookends may not have been made by the Lehman Co. The Pit-a-Pat furniture varies from 3/4" to 1" to one foot in scale. The dining room table and chair are Tudor in style. Much of the Pit-a-Pat furniture included working doors and drawers (chair $15, piano $50+, sideboard $35-45, clock $30, cabinet $35-45). *Private Collection.*

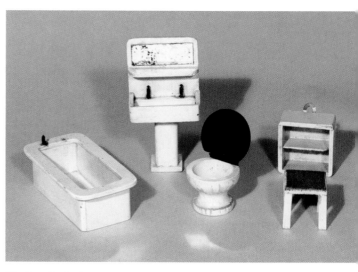

The Pit-a-Pat furniture from the bedroom has also been finished with a dark stain. It includes a bed, dresser, chair, wardrobe, and mirror. The furniture was originally marked with a paper label and an ink stamp so the furniture can be easily identified when found (bed $25, dresser, wardrobe $35-40 each, mirror $25). *Private Collection.*

The Pit-a-Pat bathroom pieces are very unique. The bathtub has a wide rim around the top, the toilet has a hinged lid, and the sink includes a mirror on top. Other pieces include a shelf and a stool (set $125-150). *Private Collection.*

Pit-a-Pat living room furniture includes upholstered sofa and chair, fireplace, clock, work basket, cutlery cabinet, cake stand, and coal scuttle (upholstered furniture $35-45, cake stand $25, cutlery cabinet $50, work basket $35, fireplace $35-45, mantel clock $20, coal scuttle $25). *Private Collection.*

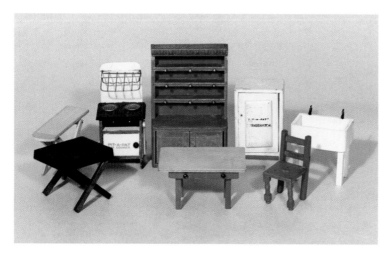

The Pit-a-Pat kitchen pieces used in the house consist of a folding table, ironing board, cooker, cabinet, refrigerator, sink (minus its draining board) and table and chair (chair $15, ironing board $20, folding table $25, table $30, cabinet and appliances $40-45 each). *Private Collection.*

Handmade Houses

Handmade childhood house of Evangeline Steinmeier. It was built by her step uncle and she received the house for Christmas in 1936. He decorated the outside of the house with paint, wood-burned vines, and a black oilcloth roof. Her step grandparents finished the inside of the house with wallpaper, furniture, and curtains (No price can be placed on sentimental value). 22" high x 19" wide x 11.25" deep. *House and photographs from the collection of Evangeline Steinmeier.*

The inside of the handmade house contains four rooms, which have been furnished as a living room, kitchen, bedroom, and bathroom. Most of the contents are original to the house. The wood furniture in three rooms is stamped "Germany" in purple. The bathroom pieces are white china stamped "Japan." The house was repapered, and vinyl tile was added in the bathroom and kitchen in 1958. *Steinmeier Collection.*

The bedroom is furnished with the original German furniture, circa 1936. It includes a bed, rocker, chair, and dresser (set $55-65). *Steinmeier Collection.*

The original German kitchen furniture, circa 1936, includes a stove, ice box, cabinet, table and chair. All of the furniture is a large 3/4" to one foot in scale (set $75+). *Steinmeier Collection.*

The original "china" bathroom pieces were made in Japan. The same set was sold by them for decades. The crocheted bathroom rug was made by the owner's step grandmother in 1936. *Steinmeier Collection.*

Boxed set of German wood furniture like that used for furnishing the living room of the Steinmeier house in 1936. The set was made with and without the "light and dark" wood trim along the edges of the furniture ($75+ boxed). *Photograph by Suzanne Silverthorn.*

The original German living room furniture from 1936 included a radio and piano as well as a sofa, chair, and table. *Steinmeier Collection.*

The printing on the label of the box that came with the German living room pieces reads "1 set 903/28 walnut/Doll Furniture/LIVING ROOM/Made in Germany."

Handmade A-frame wood and plywood house, circa 1930s. The unusual house almost has the look of a bird house. Even the front door carries out this theme. The house is surprisingly much larger than it looks ($250-400). 21.5" high x 25" long x 18.5" deep. *Photographs and house from the collection of Patty Cooper.*

This side of the house is also unusual with its dormer window that extends down into the side of the house. *Cooper Collection.*

The inside of the house has four rooms with glass windows. The back roof comes off to provide access to the rooms. It has been furnished as a kitchen, living room, bedroom, and bathroom. The house is furnished with scroll cut furniture from the 1910s and inexpensive German and Wilder furniture. The Wilder furniture was made by the Wilder Manufacturing Co. of St. Louis, Missouri, circa 1914-early 1920s. See *Furnished Dollhouses* page 70 for more information about Wilder furniture. *Cooper Collection.*

Handmade wood house on large base, circa 1940s. The house is slightly smaller than 3/4" to one foot in scale. It has four rooms, with a garage and patio ($250-400). 14.5" high x 28" wide x 18.5" deep (at base). *Photographs and house from the collection of Patty Cooper.*

The inside of the four-room house has been furnished with 1938 3/4" to one foot scale Strombecker furniture. The furniture includes pieces for a living room, kitchen, bathroom, and bedroom. Flag dolls from the 1940s live in the house. *Cooper Collection.*

Handmade Cape Cod style house, circa 1930s. The house is open backed with only two rooms. The attic with dormer windows is not accessible ($150-250). 16" high x 19.5" wide x 16" deep. *Photographs and house from the collection of Patty Cooper.*

The inside of the house has been furnished as a living room and bedroom using unidentified small 1" to one foot scaled furniture. This furniture is pictured in the *Antique and Collectible Dollhouses* book on pages 183-184. *Cooper Collection.*

Handmade house called "New Jersey Beach House" by the owner, circa late 1930s or early 1940s. The windows open by swinging out and can be removed. The roof is also removable ($400-500+). 14.5" high x 15" wide x 35.5" deep. *Photographs and house from the collection of Bonnie Benson Hanson.*

A front porch and a back porch add interest to the house. Both porches include steps. This back view of the house also pictures the open window on the side of the house. *Hanson Collection.*

When the roof of the house is removed, access can be gained to the four rooms and a bath. The house has been furnished as a living room, bedroom, kitchen, dining room, and a partial bathroom. Most of the furniture used in the house is 3/4" to one foot scale upholstered and wood pieces made by the Kage Company located in Manchester, Connecticut from 1938-1948. *Hanson Collection.*

Kage furniture used in the "Beach" house includes these kitchen and living room pieces ($5 for smaller items up to $15-20 for larger pieces). *Hanson Collection.*

1940s

Meritoy

The metal Meritoy dollhouse, circa 1949, came with plastic window panes as well as a chimney that went up the outside of the structure. The house is marked "PRODUCT OF/ Meritoy Corporation/BOSTON, MASS." ($100-125). 14.5" high x 21" wide x 10.25" deep. *House from the collection of Judith Mosholder. Photograph by Gary Mosholder.*

Meritoy Corp. advertisement for their metal dollhouse, circa 1949. The Boston based firm marketed only this one dollhouse. In the ad, the steel house sold for $3.49 unfurnished and for $5.98 complete with fifty-two pieces of furniture and six dolls. It is not known what brand of furniture came with the house. *Photograph by Suzanne Silverthorn.*

The two-story Meritoy house contained six rooms, which included a kitchen, dining room, living room, nursery, bathroom, and bedroom. They have been furnished with Renwal plastic furniture. The advertisement stated that the house could be purchased furnished but it is not known what brand of furniture was included. Renwal furniture was sometimes sold with Play Steel houses while Ideal pieces were supplied with some of the Sears cardboard houses. *Mosholder Collection.*

Mary Frances

Dollhouse made by the Kiddie Brush & Toy Co (Susy Goose) in Jonesville, Michigan in the late 1930s. The upstairs windows are made of an early plastic type material. The house is marked on the front "Play-Valu/Doll House/Kiddie Brush & Toy Co./Jonesville, Mich. Made in U.S.A." ($75+). 19" high x 30" wide x 12" deep.

The inside of the Kiddie Brush house contains movable partitions that can be used to make either a four- or five-room house. This house has been furnished mostly with "Mary Frances Line" furniture made by the Chicago based Victory Toy Company during the mid-1940s. Most of the bathroom pieces are 1" to one foot scale Strombecker furniture. The house has been papered to cover its drab brown walls.

The Kiddie Brush house was advertised in the Chicago Mail Order Company Fall & Winter catalog for 1939-1940. The pressed wood house sold for $1.69. Miniaform furniture was pictured in the catalog to be used to furnish the house. Included were pieces for a living room, dining room, bedroom, and kitchen. The furniture sold for 45 cents for each room or $1.69 for the whole set. *From the collection of Marge Meisinger.*

The Mary Frances furniture was made of quarter inch plywood and was larger than 3/4" to one foot but not quite 1" to one foot in scale. The pieces were "chunky," similar to the larger furniture called "Grand Rapids" by collectors. The living room furniture included a sofa, coffee table, chair and foot stool, and end tables. The sofa measures 5.5" long x 2.5" deep x 2.5" high (small items $5-8, large items $15-20).

Boxed Mary Frances "Breakfast Room" pieces that included a table, four chairs, and a high chair. The boxed dining room set came with four chairs with ridges used for decoration on their backs, a table, and a sideboard (boxed set $50-65).

The bedroom has been furnished with Mary Frances pieces that include a bed, dresser, rocker, and cradle. A footstool and night stand were also pieces that came in the bedroom sets. All of the furniture was put together with brads. The dolls in the house are all painted over bisque "Made in Japan" examples (furniture $12-15 each).

These unusual metal "chunky" kitchen pieces have been used to furnish the kitchen. The doors on the appliances are functional. The faucets on the sink are missing. The sink measures 3.25" wide x 2.5" deep x 4" high. "Foreign" is printed on the backboard of the sink but the maker is unknown. Perhaps the set was made in England circa late 1940s. The handles are hard plastic. The set was also marketed in bright colors (set $150-200).

Nancy Forbes+

Nancy Forbes #501 two-room house, circa early 1940s. Its flyer says it has a front door, which is apparently missing. The house has transparent windows and two rooms accessible from the open back. The two rooms are divided by a movable partition. In advertising for the houses, it was stressed that they were easy to take apart for storage. The house originally sold for $1.00 ($100). 12" high x 16" wide x 8" deep.

The inside of the Nancy Forbes house (made by American Toy & Furniture Co. in Chicago) has been furnished with Nancy Forbes "Swedish Blonde Maple" furniture. The dolls that live in the house were made by the Flagg Doll Co. of Jamaica Plain, Massachusetts in the 1940s.

Nancy Forbes 3/4" to one foot scale Blonde Maple bedroom furniture, circa 1941. This was the larger set of nine pieces that originally sold for $1.00 ($50-65).

The larger boxed 3/4" to one foot scale Nancy Forbes living room furniture came as an eleven piece set. This set has been finished in walnut. There are no opening drawers or doors on the 3/4" set ($50-65).

Handmade House

Handmade wood house, circa 1940s. It has been decorated as a "Christmas all year" house. Included are wreaths, trees, snowmen, and snow on the "ground." Nancy Ann Storybook dolls live in the house. Several of the dolls (including the ones in the front yard) have belonged to the owner since she was a young girl. 48" wide x 35" tall (including chimney) x 15" deep. *House and photograph from the collection of Marilyn Pittman.*

The inside of the large house contains six rooms plus attic space. Both the inside and the outside of the house have been redecorated. The house has been furnished as a bathroom, nursery, bedroom, kitchen, dining room, and living room. Its furnishings are a mixture of mostly American wood furniture. *Pittman Collection.*

The living room in the handmade house features two Nancy Ann Storybook dolls and a Schoenhut piano. The two dolls were given to the owner when she was a young girl and they are wearing their original clothing. *Pittman Collection.*

Accessories

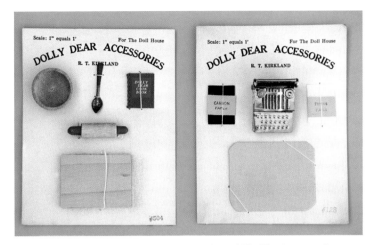

Two cards of Dolly Dear Accessories, circa late 1940s. The 1" to one foot accessories include a wood bowl, spoon, rolling pin, cookbook, and bread board. The "office" set features an upright typewriter, blotter, typing paper, and carbon paper ($15 each card).

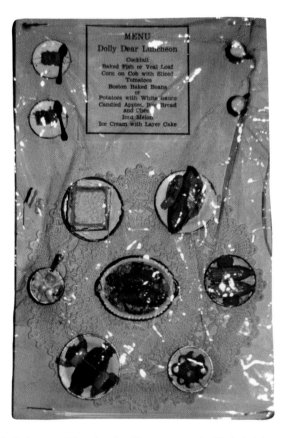

Grandmother Stover's Inc. accessories, circa 1960s. The firm was founded by John Stover in the 1940s and continued to sell miniatures into the 1970s. These small cards of accessories include a game of checkers, hot rod pieces to be used as a toy, and a fishing pole and fish ($5-8 each card).

Both Dolly Dear and Grandmother Stover accessories fit nicely into many of the dollhouses from the 1940s into the 1970s. Pictured are Dolly Dear Accessories in 1" to one foot scale, circa 1940s. The business was founded by Rossie Kirkland in Union City, Tennessee in 1928. This mint card includes an assortment of food for a complete luncheon (card $65-75). *Photograph and accessories from the collection of Ruth Petros.*

Grandmother Stover's large card of accessories, circa 1960s. Included are magazines, books, and a newspaper in a scale of 1" to one foot ($20+).

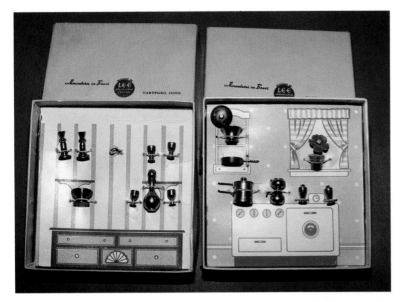

Brass dollhouse accessories in 3/4" to one foot scale produced by the Lee Manufacturing Co. in Hartford, Connecticut beginning in the late 1940s. The boxes with the solid tops appear to be early examples. Several different styles of boxes were made and it is not known how long the accessories were produced. Accessories for a dining room and a kitchen are shown ($20 each box). When smaller accessories are needed for houses from the 1940s until the 1970s, these work well. *Photograph and accessories from the collection of Roy Specht.*

Brass boxed accessory sets made by the Lee Manufacturing Co. These boxes have a "see through" front unlike the earlier designs. Included are a Breakfast Nook and a Dining Room Set ($20 each box). *Specht Collection.*

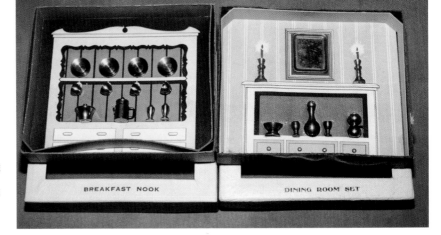

Boxed Lee sets of accessories in what appears to be a more recent box style. Included are decanter and fireplace sets ($20 each box). *Specht Collection.*

Two boxed Lee accessory sets to be used in a dollhouse living room. Although the sets appear to be identical, the box styles are different. Lamps, vases, and a mirror are included in the sets ($20 each box). *Specht Collection.*

1950s

Eagle Toys

Eagle Toys Limited fiberboard house made in Montreal, Canada, circa 1950s. It is a hexagon-shaped house on casters so it can turn for easy access to its six rooms ($150-175 furnished). 7.5" high x 21" wide. *Photographs and house from the collection of Roy Specht.*

The dining room of the Eagle house is furnished with soft plastic furniture marked "Eagle Toys Ltd./Made in Canada." The furniture is in a small 3/4" to one foot scale. *Specht Collection.*

The bedroom of the hexagon Eagle house has been furnished with brown plastic Eagle furniture. *Specht Collection.*

The marked Eagle bedroom furniture includes a bed, separate "built-in" headboard, vanity and stool, dresser with mirror, chair and a lamp. The set originally came with two lamps. *Specht Collection*.

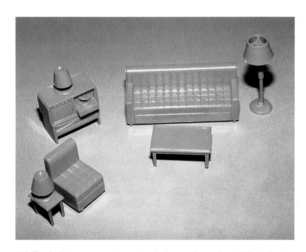

The pink Eagle living room pieces include a sofa, coffee table, television, phonograph, chair, end table, two table lamps, and a floor lamp. Another end table was also included in most sets. *Specht Collection*.

The plastic Eagle furniture for the kitchen includes a round table, four chairs, stove, refrigerator, and sink. *Specht Collection*.

The marked soft plastic Eagle dining room furniture includes a table, hutch, buffet, and four chairs. *Specht Collection*.

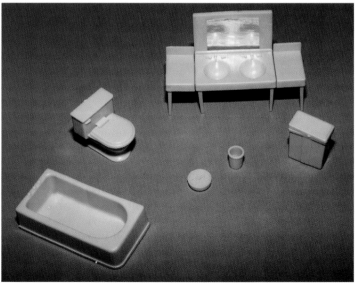

The bathrooms in the Eagle houses were furnished with a bathtub, toilet, three piece vanity with mirror, clothes hamper, scale, and wastebasket. The Eagle furniture was made in a variety of colors. *Specht Collection*.

Box for a Bungalow #821 house made by Eagle Toys Limited in Montreal, Canada, circa 1950s. The house came with patented plastic hinges that were supposed to allow assemblage of the house in thirty seconds. The retail price still marked on the box is $7.88.

The Eagle Bungalow was made of a lightweight masonite material and came on a base painted green to simulate grass. A wood chimney was also included (MIB $100). 9" high x 32" wide X 16" deep. *Photographs by Suzanne Silverthorn.*

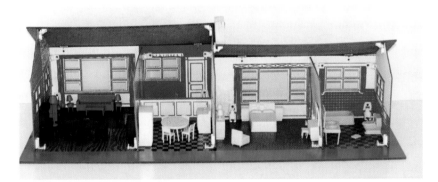

The inside of the Bungalow included four rooms plus a front hall. It came furnished with soft plastic furniture marked "Eagle Toys Ltd./Made in Canada." The furniture included pieces for a living room, dining room, kitchen, bedroom, and bathroom. The pieces are in a small 3/4" to one foot scale.

Boxed set of plastic "Cheerio" furniture made exactly like the 3/4" to one foot Jaydon plastic furniture first marketed in the United States during the mid 1940s. "Cheerio" can be seen in small blue print under "PLASTIC FURNITURE." The furniture was sold in Canada circa 1950s (boxed set $40-45). *Photograph and furniture from the collection of Roy Specht.*

Ralston Industries

Rallhouse Dollhouse, circa 1950, manufactured by Ralston Industries, located in Seattle, Washington. This circular dollhouse was built on a turntable to make it easier to access its six rooms. The chimney also served as a handle to lift the house. It is made of fiberboard and wood. The house originally came with forty pieces of plastic furniture (mostly Ideal and Renwal). It sold for $19.95 ($300+). 19" high x 20" in diameter. *House from the collection of Marcie Tubbs. Photographs by Bob Tubbs.*

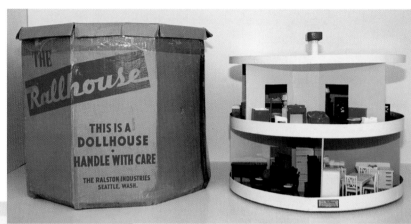

The Rallhouse has been furnished with a combination of 3/4" to one foot scaled plastic Plasco, Renwal, Best Plastics, and other hard plastic furniture of the period. Plasco outdoor furniture has been used to make a porch on the second floor of the house. *Tubbs Collection.*

Unusual Ideal plastic pink and blue kitchen furniture is featured in the kitchen. *Tubbs Collection.*

Best Plastics Corporation made several pieces in this child's room, including the bunk beds and ladder. *Tubbs Collection.*

Flagg Dolls

"Flagg Flexible Play Dolls" made by the Flagg Doll Co. of Jamaica Plain, Massachusetts beginning around 1948. The bendable dolls were made of soft plastic. They were designed by Sheila Markham Flagg. The business was sold in 1973 and was eventually closed in 1985. A variety of dollhouse size dolls were made, including a cowboy, cowgirl, nurse, pilgrims, policeman, Indians, and dollhouse family dolls (original mint $25-50 each, depending on costume and size). *Photograph and dolls from the collection of Linda Boltrek.*

Early flyer that came with boxed Flagg dolls. It lists a variety of different dolls including "Colored Maids and Cooks." *Boltrek Collection.*

Examples of Flagg dolls made with dark skin, which were to be used as dollhouse maids and cooks. Because they are harder to find, they are more expensive examples of Flagg dolls ($50+ each). *Boltrek Collection.*

A dark skin set of Flagg dolls. Included are a father, mother, little girl, little boy, and baby dolls. In 1952 a set of father and mother (each 4.5" tall) plus boy and girl (each 3.5" tall) dolls sold for $3.75 ($150+ for dark skin family). *Boltrek Collection.*

1960s

A. Barton & Co.

Barton's "Model Home" dining room furniture, circa 1970. The small wood 3/4" to one foot scale furniture featured a table, four chairs, and a sideboard with moving parts. This same line included pieces for a kitchen, bathroom, living room, and nursery. English Grecon dolls live in the Hobbies house. They have armature type bodies with embroidered hair, painted features, and metal feet. The adults are 3.5" tall (furniture $40+ set, dolls $30 each).

English "Hobbies" house, circa 1960s. The house was made from a pattern supplied by the English *Hobbies Weekly* magazine. The firm also sold the metal Romside windows, front door, and garage door used on this house ($250+). 18.5" high x 29.5" wide x 10.5" deep.

The "upholstered" living room pieces were produced by Barton, circa late 1960s or early 1970s. The desk is marked with the Dol-Toi circle sticker circa 1960s and the ABC on the face of the grandfather clock indicates it was made by A. Barton & Co.

The inside of the Hobbies house contains four rooms plus two halls. The stairs have been removed to provide space for the dining room furniture. The inside of the house was originally white but it has been papered to provide a more interesting background for the English Dol-Toi and Barton furniture. The pieces are mostly in a small 3/4" to one foot scale. The fireplaces in the house were probably also Hobbies products. The house has been furnished as a kitchen (mostly Dol-Toi), bathroom ("Rutland" sold by Dol-Toi), bedroom (mixture of Barton and Dol-Toi), dining room (Barton), and living room (mixture of Barton and Dol-Toi). See *Antique and Collectible Dollhouses* for more photographs of Dol-Toi and Barton furniture (furniture $8-20 each).

Dol-toi

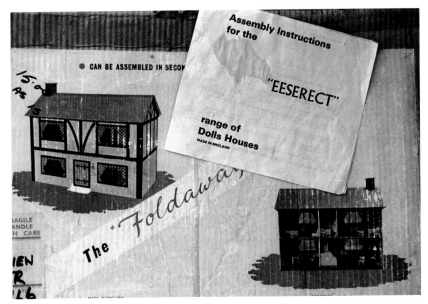

Box and instructions for the English "EESERECT" Foldaway Doll House, circa late 1960s. The house could be assembled in seconds, according to the advertising.

The EESERECT house is made of lightweight masonite with curtains and window panes printed on the clear plastic windows. The chimney is missing ($100 with box). 15" high x 20" wide x 10" deep.

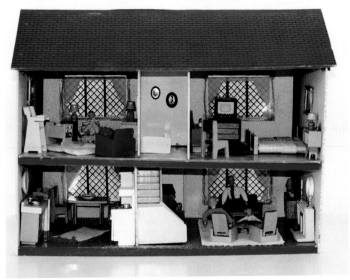

The inside of the English house has four rooms plus an upstairs hall. The red and blue floors add color to the house. The walls are a combination of light and bright yellow. The house has been furnished with a combination of English Dol-Toi and Barton furniture ranging in size from 1/2" to 3/4" to one foot in scale. A set of small scale (father 4") German Caco dolls live in the house. They are circa early 1970s.

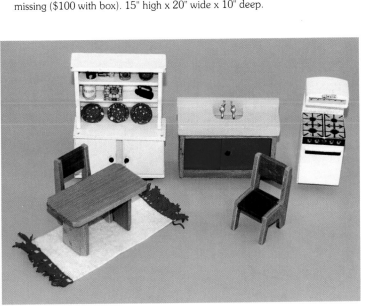

These Dol-Toi wood pieces (circa 1960s) furnish the kitchen. They include a cabinet, sink, and stove from the Dol-Toi kitchen line and a table and chairs from the dining room set. The doors are functional. Most of the pieces are marked with a round paper Dol-Toi paper label (kitchen items $12-15 each, table and two chairs $20-25 set).

Unusual Dol-Toi furniture used in the living room and bedroom of the house. The chairs are adjustable so the dolls can lean back and relax while they enjoy the "fire" in the fireplace. The books in the bookcase were also products of Dol-Toi. The furniture and plaster fireplace are marked with the round Dol-Toi tags. The Caco mother doll sits in the "recliner" (each furniture item $12-15, set of four dolls $50-60).

Boxed set of Dol-Toi wood dining room furniture, circa mid 1970s. The box reads "CONDOR/Hand crafted in rural England." This set was evidently made after the Dol-Toi firm was sold in the mid 1970s. Although the pattern of the sideboard and table appears to be the same as those sold in the 1960s, no finish has been applied and the furniture feels rough to the touch (boxed set $35).

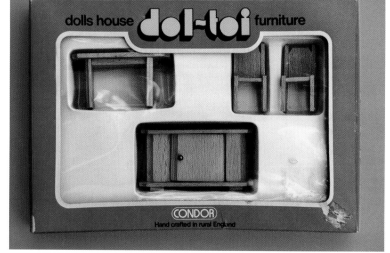

The back of the Dol-Toi box of furniture pictures other sets available from CONDOR. Included were pieces made for a living room, dining room, kitchen, bedroom, and bathroom.

Louis Marx

Louis Marx & Co. marketed a Blondie cardboard "Flip Open" dollhouse in 1968. The house included advertising that took advantage of its tie-in to the Blondie comic strip drawn by Chic Young. *Photographs and house from the collection of Roy Specht.*

The Blondie house is marked "Louis Marx & Co., Inc./ Glen Dale, W. VA./MCMLXVIII." *Specht Collection.*

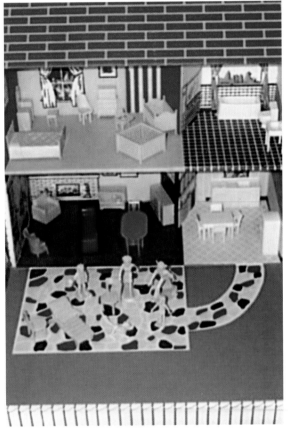

The inside of the house included four rooms. The package came complete with plastic Marx furniture to furnish a living room, dining room, bedroom, nursery, bathroom, and kitchen, and patio. *Specht Collection.*

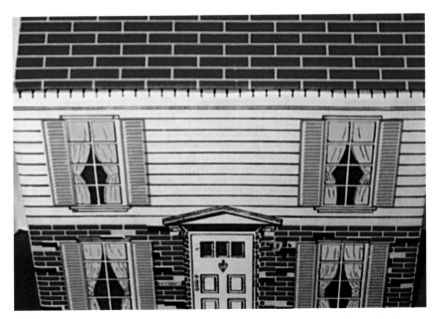

The front of the Blondie house pulled down to form a patio. A carrying handle was built in to the roof. *Specht Collection.*

The figures that came with the house represented the Blondie characters from the comic strip. Included were Blondie, Dagwood, Alexander, Cookie, and Daisy the dog. Because of the comic strip connection, this house is very collectible (Mint $600-700). *Specht Collection.*

Both the inside and the outside of the Marx Blondie house are very colorful. The 1/2" to one foot scale regular Marx plastic furniture made for a nursery and bedroom are used to furnish the upstairs bedroom. *Specht Collection.*

The kitchen is furnished with a plastic sink, stove, refrigerator, table and four chairs. All of the furniture came from Marx's regular line. *Specht Collection.*

The regular Marx dining room and living room 1/2" to one foot scale plastic pieces furnish the living room. *Specht Collection.*

Marx Little Hostess Tiny Furniture clear plastic house and furniture. It is a hard plastic, suitcase style house with eight rooms and a printed cardboard insert. The small furniture and figures are glued down ($40-50). 7.5" high x 2.5" wide x 5.25" long. *House from the collection of Marcie Tubbs. Photographs by Bob Tubbs.*

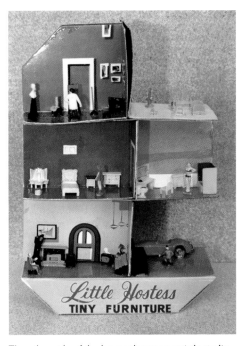

The other side of the house shows an artist's studio, the nursery, bedroom, bathroom, living room, and the garage. *Tubbs Collection.*

This side of the house features a nursery, deck, library, kitchen, garage, and dining room. The scale of the house is 1/8" to one foot. *Tubbs Collection.*

Close up of the bedroom, bathroom, and living room showing some of the "people" in the house, including a girl, bathing beauty, and grandmother. *Tubbs Collection.*

F.A.O. Schwarz

Wood and hardboard house featured in the F.A.O. Schwarz Christmas catalog for several years in the 1960s. The house sold for $35 in 1966. It has a "fieldstone" front, shutters, window boxes, clear plastic windows and a swinging door. A platform for the house could also be purchased for an additional $10.95. It included patio furniture and a simulated flagstone walk (furnished house as shown $300+). 23" high x 37" wide x 16.5" deep.

The inside of the house contains six rooms with movable interior partitions. It has been furnished with the furniture shown in the Schwarz catalogs to be used with the house. Included were 1" to one foot scale rooms of living room, dining room, kitchen, bedroom, nursery, and bathroom furniture. The furniture was produced in Germany but the house was made in the United States. In 1963, the sets of furniture were priced from $5.00 to $6.95 for each room.

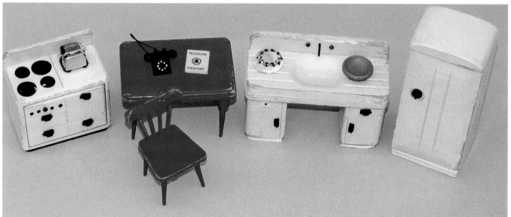

The kitchen, bathroom, and nursery sets pictured in various Schwarz catalogs included two different examples of furniture for each of these rooms. This kitchen probably dates from an earlier line. The table and chair are the same but the stove, sink, and refrigerator are a little more old fashioned than the ones pictured in the 1966 catalog. The doors on the stove and refrigerator are functional.

The wood dining room furniture sold for $5 in the Schwarz catalog. It included a table, four chairs, sideboard, serving cart, and accessories. The 1" to one foot scale furniture was made in Germany.

The German dining room furniture is very much like the 1" to one foot scale walnut furniture produced by the American Strombecker firm beginning in 1938. Strombecker pieces are pictured on the upper level while the German furniture is shown at the bottom.

The same set of German dining room furniture pictured in its original F.A.O. Schwarz box. The 1" to one foot scaled furniture sold for $5 in 1966. Besides the basic pieces, the set included two candlesticks, two potted plants, and a bird sculpture ($125-150). *Photograph and furniture from the collection of Patty Cooper.*

Pieces of the German nursery set that originally came with this Schwarz house looked exactly like the Strombecker 1" scale furniture first manufactured in 1938. The German furniture is on the left (with the missing door).

The bedroom in the Schwarz house was furnished with two beds, night stand, vanity, bench, bureau, two lamps, and a clock. This design is also very similar to the Strombecker bedroom pieces first sold in 1938. The Strombecker line is pictured at the top of the photograph and the German pieces are at the bottom. Both bureaus have two drawers that open as one unit. The mirror has been replaced on the German vanity.

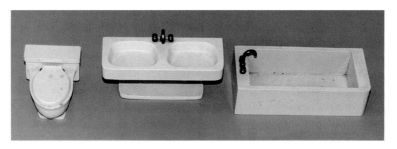

This set of German bathroom furniture, with a double sink, has been used to furnish the bathroom in the Schwarz house. It was pictured in the Schwarz 1966 catalog, priced at $4.50, and also included a wall cabinet with a hinged glass front and a stool.

The living room is furnished with German furniture like that pictured in the Schwarz 1966 catalog. Besides the pieces shown, a footstool, floor lamp, and plant stand were also included in the set. German Erna Meyer dolls, circa 1970s, live in the house.

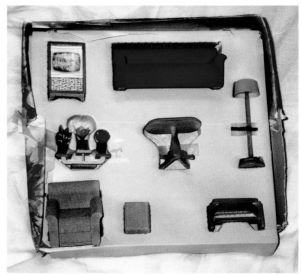

Boxed set of German living room furniture carried by F.A.O. Schwarz to be used to furnish their six-room house. The sofa, chair, and foot stool are flocked ($125-150). *Photograph and furniture from the collection of George Mundorf.*

"Peasant" dollhouse imported from West Germany by F.A.O. Schwarz and featured for many years in the firm's Christmas catalogs. The furnished house sold for $59.50 in their 1963 catalog. It came with twenty-five pieces of decorated "Peasant" style furniture. The flower pots have been added to this house. The wood house included a balcony and opening doors (furnished $250+). 17" high x 29" wide x 16" deep.

The inside of the "Peasant" house featured three large rooms furnished with colorfully decorated wood furniture. The inside of the house was finished in natural wood and curtains were provided for the six windows. Many of the pieces of furniture that came with the house were duplicates. A cuckoo clock was originally part of the furnishings. The one pictured is a replacement.

The West German furniture that was to be used to furnish the house was in a large 1" to one foot scale. The bedroom furniture included two canopy beds, two wardrobe pieces, two low chests, and two chairs. All of the furniture featured opening doors and drawers.

The kitchen was to be furnished with a table, four chairs, cabinet, stove, and chest. The newer accessories did not come with the house.

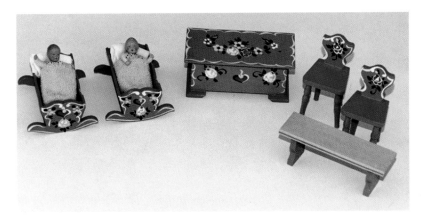

The west German house's furnishings also included two cradles, a blue opening chest, bench (also supplied in rose color), and four blue chairs. The German Caco twin dolls did not come with the house.

Although these three pieces of West German furniture were not part of the original furnishings, they are from the peasant line of furniture and look very nice in the house. The "upholstery" matches that on the canopy beds. The rocker, settee, and stand are all decorated in the same manner as the other furniture (set $50+).

This set of German Caco Peasant dolls is similar to one that was featured in the F.A.O. Schwarz Christmas catalog in 1963 to be used with the house. They sold separately for $4.50 but with their sizes ranging from 2.25" to 4", they are really too small for the larger scaled house and furniture. These dolls have plastic heads and hands and date from the 1970s. The Caco girl doll sitting in the kitchen of the West German house is a better size. She measures 3.5" tall (set $30+).

The West German "Peasant" furniture was also offered in box sets. Pictured are both bedroom and kitchen pieces. *Photograph and furniture from the collection of Ruth Petros.*

Spot-on Tri-ang

Box for a Tri-ang Spot-On Jennys Home set, circa 1965. Included were two large rooms, one small room, chimney, seven pieces of furniture, two lamps, and a Jenny doll. The box is labeled "JR-105. Made in Northern Ireland by Spot-On Models Limited. Planned in association with Homes and Gardens Magazine. A Tri-ang Product." Jennys Home was first introduced in 1965. Production continued, with some changes, until approximately 1970. The English Tri-ang firm ceased operations in 1971.

The Jennys Home living room pieces included a sofa, wing chair, occasional chair, bookcase, desk, floor lamp, and table lamp. The lamp could be made to light with the use of a battery concealed in the chimney. The Spot-On Tri-ang Jennys Home furniture was made of "high-impact Polystyrene with die cast parts adding strength and durability," according to the firm's advertising. The furniture was listed as 1/16 in scale. The drawers and doors are functional.

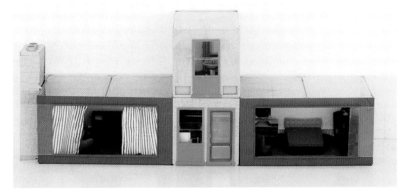

Spot-On Jennys Home and furniture, an English Tri-ang product. The houses could be assembled using a variety of large and small rooms. This model includes two large rooms, two small rooms, and a chimney. The large rooms are 6" high x 11" wide x 8" deep. The smaller rooms measure 6" high x 5.5" wide x 8" deep. The doors and windows opened on the various rooms. Doors were removable so entry could be made from one room to another. An extra room and a few more pieces of furniture have been added to the basic set (this set with furniture and box $550).

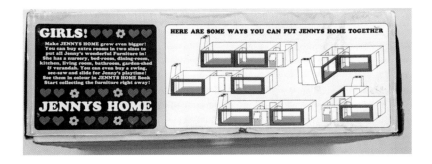

The outside of the Jennys Home box pictures various ways to add additional clear plastic rooms to the house to make it larger.

The Jennys Home bedroom included a bed, vanity, bench, and wardrobe (not pictured). The bathroom sink came with this Jennys Home set, but no bathtub or toilet was included. A bedroom chest was also sometimes offered. The television and red chair could also be used in the living room.

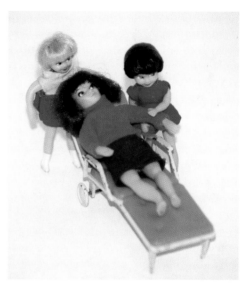

The Jenny doll that came with the house is a 3.5" tall vinyl bendable doll, with molded hair and painted features, wearing a removable red dress and underwear. She is marked "Made in Hong Kong" on the back. Other dolls could be purchased to be used in the Jenny sets. They included mother, father, brother, and baby dolls as well as a Jenny with a wig instead of molded hair. Pictured along with the molded hair Jenny are the mother doll (4.5" tall) and the Jenny doll with a wig (3.5" tall). Both wear their original clothing. The J1118 Sun Lounge chair made of metal and plastic is also shown. A covered glider set #J027, called a Garden Hammock, was also made (dolls with wigs $20 each, lounge $25+).

The basic Jennys Home kitchen set featured a stove, built-in sink, table, and two chairs. Other pieces including a refrigerator, cabinet, and washing machine could be purchased separately. The refrigerator and washing machine can be expensive to buy since they did not come with the basic sets and are, therefore, harder to find. Various accessories including the fish on a plate and the pots and pans also came with the sets.

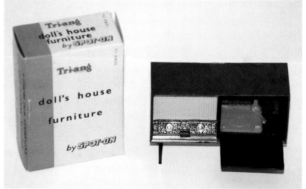

Tri-ang Spot-On Philips Radiogram #1020 with its original box. The door opens to reveal a phonograph. The bottom and legs of the piece are metal while the rest is made of plastic. The Jennys Home Spot-On furniture could also be purchased separately in individual boxes so additional furniture could be acquired to furnish the available rooms. The furniture is not marked (MIB radio-phonograph $30+).

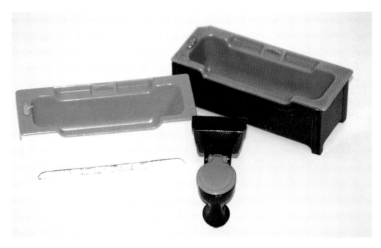

The bathroom sets included a toilet, sink, bathtub, stool, and bathmat. Two different bathtubs were produced. The white tub was made with the upper parts of plastic while only the bottom is metal. The black tub features metal on the outside with only the inside and top decorative piece made of plastic. The toilet is all metal except for its lids, which are plastic (each piece $25+).

The Jennys Home nursery set came with a drop side crib, playpen, baby bath and stand, Noah's Ark, and rocking horse. The buggy could be purchased separately. The playpen, baby's bath and Noah's Ark are not pictured. The baby items are some of the hardest pieces to find and may cost $50-100 or more each, especially the buggy. *Photograph and furniture from the collection of Liz Cathcart.*

These Spot-On Divan Beds date from 1961 before the Jennys Home line was issued. They are very hard to find. Pictured with them is the broom closet, also available in 1961. It included the closet, ladder, dustpan and brush, broom and a non-electrical sweeper. The set was updated for the Jennys Home line when an electric sweeper replaced the old model (not enough examples to determine price). *Cathcart Collection.*

The outside of the Jennys Home box pictures many of the unusual pieces of furniture that could be purchased separately. In addition, a dining room package was issued that included a table, four chairs, sideboard, and floor lamp. Besides those items, a slide, teeter totter, and swing were marketed as part of a Playtime set. Tools were also made for Jenny and her family. They included a lawnmower, roller, wheel barrow, rake, and shovel.

1970s

Blue Box

The inside of the Blue Box house has four rooms and a hall. There is also a stairway from the first to second floor. The furniture is in approximately 1/2" to one foot in scale. It is made of plastic as are the "people." Furniture was provided for a living room, kitchen, bedroom, and bathroom.

Blue Box plastic house and box, circa mid to late 1970s. The writing on the box reads "BLUE BOX TOYS/DOLL HOUSE/WITH FURNITURE/AND 4-PIECE FAMILY SET/32 PCS." It was made in Hong Kong and distributed by BLUE BOX in New York City. The plastic house can be taken apart for storage. It has some sliding plastic windows and an opening front door (MIB $25). Base 9.5" high (not including chimney), 19.5" wide x 9" deep.

Pictured is the Blue Box furniture for the living room and kitchen. The pieces are brightly colored. The "family" relaxes in the chairs. The piano and bench from the living room is not pictured. Most of the furniture is marked "Made in Hong Kong."

"Blue Box" Dream House boxed plastic furniture, circa 1970s. The design of the furniture appears to be loosely based on the Ideal Petite Princess pieces. The scale is approximately 1/2" to one foot. A sticker on each box reads "BRINNCO/Pittsburg, PA./Made in HONG KONG." The furniture is marked "BLUE BOX/MADE IN HONG KONG" (three boxes $20-25).

Brumberger

Brumberger Colonial House advertised in the Sears Christmas catalog in 1975. The Brumberger Company, located in Brooklyn, New York, apparently purchased the T. Cohn firm during this time. They marketed several known T. Cohn products under their name. The plastic furniture for this house was made using the Superior (T. Cohn) molds.

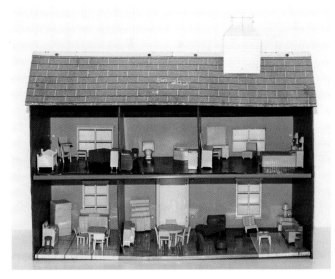

The inside of the Colonial house includes five rooms, which are furnished with 1/2" to one foot scaled plastic furniture. The furniture is the small "Superior" line sold earlier with T. Cohn houses. The house includes a kitchen, combination dining room-living room, nursery, bathroom, and bedroom.

The Brumberger house was made of colorfully decorated hardboard with plastic windows and chimney and unusual decorated steel floors. The furnished house sold for $13.97 ($50+ furnished). 20" high x 24" wide x 10" deep.

A similar Brumberger house was made in a larger size. This house included an extra window on the lower story and a different color scheme. It appears that the same tiny Superior plastic furniture was included for use in furnishing six rooms. The living room and dining room were combined into one room so the house contained only five rooms. The boxed house dates from 1978 (MIB $75-100). 23.5" high x 30" wide x 13" deep. *Photograph and house from the collection of Evangeline Steinmeier.*

A similar Brumberger house included red shutters, different shrubbery, and no window over the door. 23.5" high x 30" wide x 13" deep. *Photograph and house from the collection of Evangeline Steinmeier.*

Collectors have known for years that T. Cohn, Inc., of Brooklyn, New York, produced this metal dollhouse furnished with 1/2" to one foot scale plastic furniture. It is surprising to discover that the same house was also marketed at a later date by the Brumberger Co., also located in Brooklyn, New York. It appears that Brumberger took over the assets of T. Cohn, probably by purchase. This metal house also came with the small Superior plastic furniture (MIB $100+). 13.5" high x 23" wide x 9.5" deep. *Photograph and house from the collection of Roy Specht.*

Three other models of Brumberger houses dating from the 1970s. More information about the Chalet and the Town House can be found in the *Furnished Dollhouses* book. The Brumberger house with the blue roof is decorated with the same stone pattern as the Chalet house. It has unusual dormer type windows. The house contains four rooms with a patio (unfurnished house $40+). 11" tall x 13" wide x 9.5" deep. *Photograph and houses from the collection of Roy Specht.*

Hall's Lifetime Toys

1965

Hall's LifeTime Toys Catalog, dated 1965. The Hall's firm was located in Chattanooga, Tennessee from 1942 until the late 1970s. The large Plantation dollhouse was featured on the cover. It was listed as "new" in the 1965 catalog. *Photographs and catalog from the collection of Becky Norris.*

Unlike the later Hall's houses this older model did not include wallpapered walls. The copy in the booklet states that the walls were painted pink and blue. The upstairs decoration is probably original while the downstairs has been repainted. The house includes six rooms, mostly furnished with Hall's wood furniture. The canopy bed comes from the more expensive line of Hall's furniture. This house has electric lights that operate with a battery. By the 1970s, the basic design of this house was changed to include smaller windows containing clear plastic inserts printed with curtains. The shape of the upstairs oval window was altered to match the other windows. *Norris Collection.*

Early Hall's Lifetime Toys Plantation house #06 from 1965. The booklet that came with the house pictured the house with no windows but the house did originally have a balcony under the upstairs curved window. The house was made of wood and hardboard and included hardwood grained floors. It came with a set of porch furniture which included green chairs, styled like the regular living room chairs. The information with the house also pictures the cheaper line of Hall's furniture priced at $4 for each set. The retail price on the house was $30 (missing balcony $250). 25.25" high x 27.5" wide x 12" deep (17.75" with porch). *Norris Collection.*

Besides making dollhouses and 1" to one foot scaled furniture, the Hall firm also produced a line of larger furniture to be used with 8"-10" size dolls during the late 1950s and 1960s. Included were pieces for a living room, dining room, bedroom, and kitchen. (Most of the kitchen furniture appeared to be printed on the wall in this advertisement.) The firm also marketed a "Fold-Away Doll House" constructed of PlyVeneer with lithographed walls and floors. This house was to be used with the large furniture. The ad shown here probably dates from the late 1950s or early 1960s when the 8"-10" dolls were so popular. The dollhouses came in either one-room, two-room, or four-room models, priced at $3.95, $5.95, and $9.95 respectively. The one-room model measured 17.25" high x 20" wide x 20" deep. *Photograph by Suzanne Silverthorn.*

The 1965 Hall's catalog featured a large scaled "Suburban House" #203 to be used with 8"-12" size dolls. The copy stated that the house was the most popular Hall item in 1964. The two-story, open back house had three rooms and sold for $25. The house was unfurnished but did include curtains. 24" high x 40" wide x 18" deep. *Norris Collection.*

The 1965 Hall's catalog pictured many pieces of furniture in various sizes. Two different living room sets (modern and upholstered) were shown to be used with 8"-12" dolls. They sold for $9-10 a set. Dining room furniture, priced at $10 per set, was made in both Colonial and modern styles. The Colonial bedroom furniture came as a set for $12.00. Other pieces could be purchased individually, including a rocker for $2.50. All of the furniture was to be used with 8"-12" dolls. The consumer had the choice of Early American or cherry finish on the wood. *Norris Collection.*

The Hall's catalog also pictured furniture for infant dolls in 1965. Most of the items were designed for the 8" baby dolls then popular. Included were high chairs, shooflys, cribs, clothes racks, and wardrobes. Most of these sold for $2.50-4.00 each in colors of white or pink. *Norris Collection.*

The same 1965 Hall's catalog advertised a town house that could be purchased furnished or unfurnished. The furniture to be used in this house is similar to that pictured in *Antique and Collectible Dollhouses*, except for a different dining room hutch, television, baby dresser, and the addition of a shoofly. The unfurnished house sold for $20. *Norris Collection.*

Cape Cod Manor House #106D made by Hall's Lifetime Toys of Chattanooga, Tennessee, circa 1972. The house was made of wood and hardboard with lauan mahogany plywood floors. In 1972 the house was priced at $80 ($400). 27" high x 39" wide x 15" deep.

The inside of the Hall's Cape Cod Manor House included six rooms that have been furnished with Hall's 1" to one foot scale wood furniture. The kitchen and bathroom contain pieces from the more expensive "Mini-Line" of furniture, while the rest of the rooms are furnished with the cheaper basic furniture. The inside of the house may have been repapered.

The living room includes the original built-in bookcases and fireplace as well as the Hall living room furniture and mostly newer accessories. Newer German Caco dolls live in the house.

The bedroom of the Cape Cod house is big enough to accommodate two of the large Hall beds plus the night stand, rocker, and dresser.

Hall's #1028 Cottage house, circa early 1970s. It is wood and hardwood construction. The house came with two movable partitions so it could be used as a two- or four-room house. The windows are clear plastic with curtains printed on ($100+). 16" high x 24" wide x 12" deep. *Photographs and house from the collection of Becky Norris.*

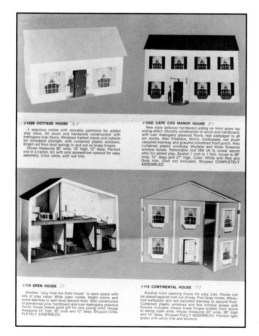

This page from a 1970s Hall catalog pictures four houses from the Hall Lifetime Toy Line. Included were a Cottage House, Cape Cod Manor House, Open House, and Continental house. *Catalog from the collection of Lois Freeman.*

The inside of this Hall's Cottage has no partitions although it has been furnished as four rooms. The furniture is a mixture of Hall's 1" to one foot scaled furniture and other wood furniture of the era. The bathroom is ceramic. *Norris Collection.*

Lynnfield-Block House-Sonia Messer

"Town House Doll House Packet" issued by Craft Patterns, circa late 1960s to early 1970s. The pattern came from the Craft Pattern Studio, Elmhurst, Illinois. It was designed by A. Neely Hall. The packet included plans to make the five-room house as well as plastic window panes and flowers for the flower boxes.

The house contained five windows and an opening door on the front, with no windows on the sides ($200). 39" high x 24" wide x 13.5" deep.

The front of the house opens in two sections to reveal five large rooms. The house has been furnished with 1" to one foot scale Lynnfield (most of kitchen and bedroom), Block House Columbia (dining room, piano, and secretary), and Sonia Messer (upholstered living room furniture and wood end tables) furniture. The bathroom pieces, which are original to the house, appear to be handmade. German Caco dolls in 1" to one foot scale live in the house. The boy and girl, with composition heads and metal hands and feet, are wearing pajamas.

The handmade bathroom pieces included a bathtub, sink, toilet, and medicine cabinet (on the wall). Bent metal was used for the spouts and faucets were made of screws and heavy thumb tacks. Doors were drawn on and do not function. Heavy staples were used for the hinges and nails were used for the toilet handle and the knob on the cabinet door.

B. Shackman & Co.

Handmade wood house, circa 1970s. The front of the house has five glass windows, a functional front door, and interesting architectural accents. It has been mounted on rollers for easy access to its opening back. A Shackman wood bench is on the front porch (house $125). Platform 30.5" wide x 18.5" deep. House 20" high x 26.5" wide x 13" deep.

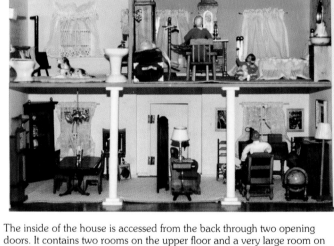

The inside of the house is accessed from the back through two opening doors. It contains two rooms on the upper floor and a very large room on the lower story. The house has been furnished mostly with Shackman furniture. B. Shackman & Co. was a wholesale importing firm located in New York City. The company was founded in Wilkes Barre, Pennsylvania in the 1890s by Bertha Shackman. Eventually the business moved to New York City when Bertha's four sons ran the firm. In the 1970s, the company was still managed by descendents when their catalogs featured many pieces of 1" to one foot scaled furniture as well as dolls and accessories.

Most of the Shackman products were made in Japan but some were produced in Germany or Taiwan. All of the items carry a Shackman copyright on the box and/or on a sticker. Pictured are a wood bench, wind-up musical piano, miniature library books, pitcher and bowl, and soft metal wall sconce. Everything is in a 1" to one foot scale. All of these items were pictured in B. Shackman's catalog in 1973 (piano $20-30, bench $8-10, accessories $5-15).

Much of the Japanese furniture sold by Shackman was made of cherry wood. This includes the wardrobe pictured here. Other items shown are a towel holder, clothes rack, trunk, and sewing machine ($15-35 each).

Other Shackman products included an ice box, medicine cabinet, toothbrush and toothpaste, and a fireplace accessory set which included a tool set, billows, andirons, and a gold clock with glass dome ($5-25 each).

Shackman living room furniture in the house includes a sofa, chair and footstool, table, and screen. All were made in Japan ($15-25 each).

Additional Shackman items used to furnish the handmade house include a drop front desk, two ladder back chairs with rush seats, a wall bookcase, and a cherry umbrella and cane stand with a mirror ($10-25 each).

Other Shackman items used to furnish the house include a corner cabinet, table with extra leaf, grandfather clock, and globe on a stand ($10-25 each).

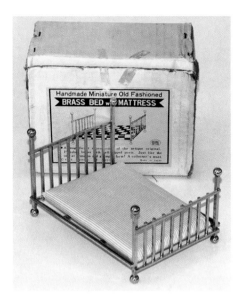

The Shackman "brass bed" appears to be larger in scale than other items marketed by the firm. It measures 7" long x 4.5" wide and was made in Japan ($25).

This German Caco family set of dolls was offered in the Shackman catalog for 1973. The dolls range in size from 3.75" to 5.5" tall. They have composition type heads, metal hands and feet, and armature bodies. Both the mother and daughter have wigs while the father and son have molded hair (MIB set $75-100).

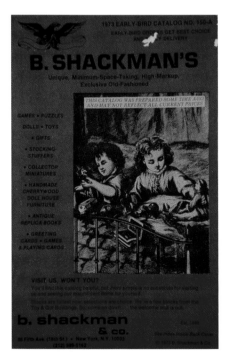

This "Porcelain Bathroom Set" consisting of three pieces was also featured in the Shackman 1973 catalog. It was made in Taiwan ($15-20).

B. Shackman & Co.'s catalog for 1973, which offered over four hundred different dollhouse items for sale. Included were accessories, furniture, and dollhouse dolls.

Chapter 2

Cardboard and Paper Dollhouses and Furniture

Cardboard and paper dollhouses are popular with many collectors because they can be stored flat and take up only a small amount of space. These houses have also been favorites of mail order companies because they came packaged unassembled and were easy to ship to customers. In addition, since these houses were very inexpensive to produce, many have been used for advertising purposes (see *American Dollhouses and Furniture From the 20th Century* for photographs and information on additional cardboard and paper houses and furniture).

Some of the houses and furniture were made of heavy paper while the more functional houses and furniture were produced using heavy cardboard. These types of houses have been on the market for nearly 150 years.

Besides houses to be assembled, several companies designed cardboard and paper houses in book form. Many of these products contained furniture and a paper doll family as part of the package. Some of the houses were to be punched out of the book and assembled while other products included only people and furniture to be removed from the book.

Although many different companies designed and sold cardboard houses and furniture, the most prolific company began business as the Warren Paper Products Co. in the early 1920s. The firm, located in Lafayette, Indiana, was originally a paper box manufacturer. The company began the manufacture of paper toys in the mid 1930s. Within a few years, the toy line was being mar-

keted under the "Built-Rite" trademark. Toys were made for both boys and girls. Included were forts, railroad stations, farms, airplanes, dollhouses, and dollhouse furniture (see *Toy Buildings* book for more information). The toys were all packaged in pieces and the consumer was expected to assemble the products after purchase. The boxes containing the different models were also used as the bases for the various buildings. Dollhouses ranged in size from one to five rooms and two lines of cardboard dollhouse furniture were made to furnish the houses. The cardboard toys went out of style in the 1950s with the coming of plastic and metal playsets and dollhouses.

Some of the other firms producing cardboard dollhouses and/or furniture in the United States include the following:

Andrews, O.B., Chattanooga, Tennessee, circa mid 1930s.
Durrel Co., Boston, Massachusetts, circa 1920s (Trixy houses and furniture).
Gable House & Carton Co., New York, circa 1914-1920s.
Grimm & Leeds Co., Camden, New Jersey, 1903.
Jayline Toys, Inc., Philadelphia, Pennsylvania, circa 1940s.
McLoughlin Brothers, New York, circa 1870-early 1900s.
Sutherland Paper Co., Kalamazoo, Michigan, circa early 1930s.
Transogram, New York and Brooklyn, circa mid 1930s.
Wayne Paper Products, Fort Wayne, Indiana, circa 1920s and early 1930s.

Dollhouse Books

Little Pet's Play House published by Sam'l Gabriel Sons & Co. of New York in 1920. This boxed set included a three-sided cardboard "house" plus dolls and toys to cut out ($75+). *Photographs and book from the collection of Sharon Barton.*

The inside of the *Little Pet's Play House* featured windows, a door, and furniture (including a dollhouse) decorating its walls. *Barton Collection.*

My Dolly's Home was published by Arts and General Publishers, Limited, in Temple, London, circa late 1920s. The book "house" was by Doris Davey after Helen Waite. It included a hall, living room, library, stairs, bedroom, child's room, bedroom, nursery, sewing room, bathroom, kitchen, and a paper doll family. The rooms in the book were ready for their paper doll family's use. No furniture needed to be added to make the house complete ($50+). *From the collection of Elaine Price.*

Our New Home #890 was published by Sam'l Gabriel Sons & Co. of New York in 1930. The story was by Susan S. Popper and the illustrations were by Helen Ohrenschall. This "house" book contains a kitchen, living room, children's room, parent's room, dining room, and garden. Furniture and paper people were also included in the package ($75). *Price Collection.*

The furniture for *Our New Home* was to be cut out and matched with the proper number in the room where it belonged. The paper dolls were to be glued to heavier paper and then cut out. The kitchen and its furniture are pictured. *Price Collection.*

My Doll's House was published by Stecher Litho. Co. of Rochester, New York in 1932. The book included a living room, bedroom, and kitchen. Like other books of its kind, the furniture was to be cut out and glued in the proper places in the rooms by matching the numbers ($65+). *Price Collection.*

House We Live In #891 was published by Sam'l Gabriel Sons and Co. of N.Y., circa early 1930s. The illustrations are by Helen E. Ohrenschall. The inside of the "house" included a living room, kitchen, dining room, bedroom, children, and a garden room. The furnishings and figures were to be cut out and glued in the proper rooms ($65+). *Price Collection.*

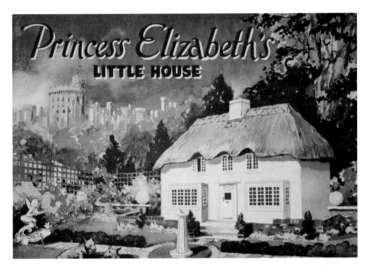

Princess Elizabeth's Little House was published by Dean & Son Limited, London, circa late 1930s. The book contains seven pages that include a house and garden to assemble. The furniture is pictured on the walls ($100+). *Photograph and book from the collection of Ruth Petros.*

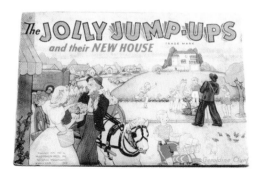

The Jolly Jump-Ups and Their New House was published by McLoughlin Bros., Inc. of Springfield, Massachusetts beginning in 1939 ($45+). *From the collection of Arliss and Gene Morris. Photograph by Gene Morris.*

The Jolly Jump-Ups book folds out into various rooms with pop-up furniture. Included were a moving day scene, kitchen, dining room, living room, bedroom, and recreation room. *Morris Collection.*

Cardboard and Paper Furniture

Advertisement for cardboard doll furniture from *Needlecraft* magazine in 1921. The furniture was a premium to be given away to subscribers who obtained four new subscriptions to the magazine. *From the collection of Mary Stuecher. Photograph by Werner Stuecher.*

The same doll furniture, in a boxed set, was published by Sam'l Gabriel Sons and Co. Perhaps this set was issued at a later date. The box included eight sheets of furniture and four rugs made of thin cardboard ($75+). *Photograph and furniture from the collection of Ruth Petros.*

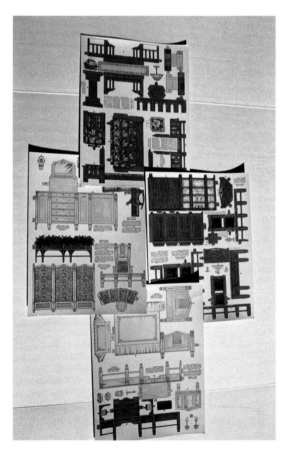

This packaged furniture appears to be the same as that offered by the *Needlecraft* magazine in 1921. The furniture was made of thin cardboard by American Colortype Co. of Chicago ($75+). *From the collection of Arliss and Gene Morris. Photograph by Gene Morris.*

These four sheets of cardboard furniture came from the Sam'l Gabriel boxed set of furniture. Included were pieces for a bedroom, living room, and dining room. *Petros Collection.*

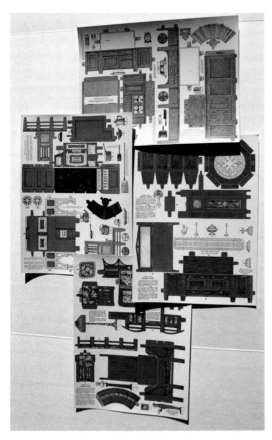

Fairy Princess Interlocking Doll Furniture, circa 1930s. The box reads, "The American Crayon Company/Sandusky, Ohio - New York/Set No. 2134 Patent Applied For." The set included four rooms of furniture: living room (orange and black), dinette (green and white), bedroom (pink and white), and kitchenette (pink and white). The pieces have never been assembled and are locked together like a jigsaw puzzle ($75+). *Photograph and furniture from the collection of Marge Powell.*

The other four sheets featured furniture for the kitchen, living room, and dining room. Four cardboard rugs were also included in the set. It is thought that this furniture was sold for many years and was still being offered in 1930. *Petros Collection.*

Right:
Let's Make Furniture published by Whitman Publishing Co. in 1934. This is a large six page book of lightweight cardboard furniture that includes pieces to furnish a dining room, bedroom, and kitchen ($60+). *Photograph and book from the collection of Ruth Petros.*

Below:
These inside pages of *Let's Make Furniture* show pieces for use in furnishing the dining room, bedroom, and kitchen along with many accessories. *Petros Collection.*

Bradley's Playhouse Furniture Cut-Outs #8248 produced by the Milton Bradley Company of Springfield, Massachusetts, circa 1920s. The set consisted of three pages of lightweight cardboard fold-up furniture. Included were items for a nursery, library, and dining room. The same company also issued a set #8249 that featured three large sheets of paper furniture to be colored, cut-out, and assembled. The sheets are marked with the McLoughlin Bros. name ($65+). *Photograph and furniture from the collection of Ruth Petros.*

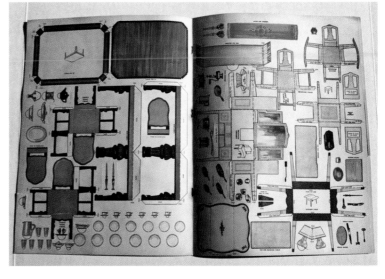

1900s

Grimm & Leeds four-room cardboard version of the "Dandy Toy House." The company was located in Camden, New Jersey and patented these houses in 1903. Several designs were made including both two-room and four-room models (see earlier books for other examples). Their houses were made to be assembled when used for play, and could be easily taken apart for storage. One of these four-room houses was advertised in the John Wanamaker holiday catalog in 1905. It was called a "Collapsible Doll House" and was priced at $2.00 ($700-750). 21" high x 19" wide X 15.5" deep. *Photograph and house from the collection of Patty Cooper.*

The inside of the Grimm & Leeds house contains four rooms with printed wood-grain floors and a tiny floral pattern on the walls. The windows have isinglass panes and green paper shades with lace trim. The exterior has lithographed stone on the first floor and fish scale shingles on the second. *Cooper Collection.*

1910s

Advertisement for thin cardboard "Dolly's Home" from *The American Woman* in 1913. The house and six paper dollies were premiums to be given to the customer when they secured two new subscriptions to the magazine. The copy does not say how many rooms the house contained. 12" high x 12" wide x 10" deep. *From the collection of Leslie and Joanne Payne.*

1920s

Package for the "Kiddies' Bungalow" sold by the Douglas Mfg. Co. of Kansas City, Missouri. The information on the envelope includes a copyright date of 1922 and the firm's address of 2615 Walnut St. *Photograph and package from the collection of Marge Powell.*

The "Kiddies' Bungalow" is made of cardboard and features an opening door in the back ($50+). 7" high x 12" wide x 9" deep. *Powell Collection.*

Boxed "Dolly's Cottage with Furniture and Dolls" produced by Charles E. Graham & Co., New York, circa 1920s ($100+). *From the collection of Arliss and Gene Morris. Photograph by Gene Morris.*

Cardboard "Dolly's Cottage," containing one room. 10" high x 14 3/4" wide x 9" deep. *Morris Collection.*

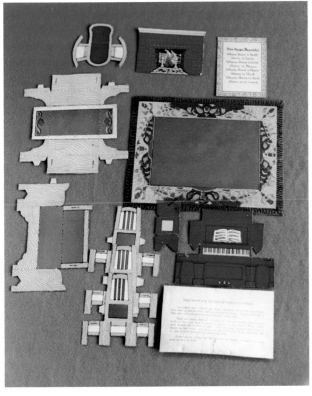

Cardboard furniture and rug that came with "Dolly's Cottage." The pieces were to be folded and slotted into place. Chubby little cardboard children were also part of the set. *Morris Collection.*

A two-story cardboard house with paper furniture was advertised in the Sears Fall and Winter catalog of 1923. The set sold for 98 cents. *From the collection of Marge Meisinger.*

Toy Makers two-room cardboard house marked 1921 as advertised in the Sears catalog for 1923 ($100+ with furniture). 14" high x 14" wide x 11 1/2" deep.

The front of the house, as well as the roof, could be removed for play. The house was furnished as a bedroom and living room with heavy paper furniture.

Besides the pieces pictured, the house originally included another rocking chair and vanity in the bedroom and a table in the living room.

Lithographed Doll Houses

09136/1. Gable Villa is about the prettiest novelty put on the market for some time, it is in the form of a two-storey semi-bungalow, four gables, with windows and awnings, lower windows equipped with shutters and awnings; opening in back to put in toys, green lawn base; size over all 11⅜x14¾x9¾ inches; each in printed envelope, comes flat; 1 dozen in package. .... Doz. **$4.00**

09136/2. The Bungalow. Built on the same principle as 09136/1, but representing the newest bungalow type of one-storey residence. Lithographed in red and green, with front lawn base; size set up 16x10½x8 inches; each comes flat in printed envelope; 1 dozen in package. .... Doz. **$4.00**

Cardboard houses advertised in the Nerlich & Co. catalog in 1924. The Bungalow came in an 8" x 16" x 10 1/2" size. It was lithographed in red and green. Both houses were made by the Gable House and Carton Co. in New York. *From the collection of Marge Meisinger.*

The original package for the Gable Villa house showed no awnings on the windows. This house, without awnings, had been advertised as early as 1915. At that time the house sold for only 25 cents. *Photograph and package from the collection of Evangeline Steinmeier.*

The Gable Villa house from the early 1920s had a slightly different look than the houses from 1915. Awnings had been added and the porch was modified. The back opening house came on a green lawn base ($65-75). 9 3/4" high x 14 3/4" wide x 11 3/8" deep. *Steinmeier Collection.*

Lightweight cardboard No. 151 house made by CEL-Met Products in Rochester, New York in 1923. The full name of the parent company was Cellu-metal Corp. The house was to be assembled by folding on dotted lines and using prongs. Several similar inexpensive houses, packaged in envelopes, were marketed during the mid 1920s ($50+). 9" high x 16" wide x 8" deep. *Photograph and house from the collection of Sharon Barton.*

Another similar thin cardboard house was made by the Art Toy Co. in Rochester, New York in 1925. It included a house, driveway, garage, and car. The package is marked "No 1" and "Patent Applied For" ($45+). 8" high x 7" wide. *Photograph and house from the collection of Ruth Petros.*

LePageville House, circa 1920s. This house was one of a series used to advertise LePage Glue. It is the No. 3 Cape Cod Cottage. The others included Dutch Colonial, Georgian Colonial, and Colonial. Each house came in an envelope and was priced at 10 cents ($50+). *From the collection of Arliss and Gene Morris. Photograph by Gene Morris.*

LePageville #4 Colonial House in its original envelope. All of these lightweight cardboard houses were very fragile and are hard to find in excellent condition ($50+). *Morris Collection.*

Trixytoy house like the one pictured in the Colson advertisement. Although the roof was originally red, it has faded through the years. The house came with its original directions for assembly and the printed information stated that a patent had been applied for. Several of these houses were made in various sizes and slightly different designs. They were made by the Durrel Company in Boston, Massachusetts ($125+). 13" high (not including chimney) x 19" wide x 12" deep.

She Needed a Telephone

So does any little girl who likes to play house. It is brightly colored and has a real bell. You'll like it when you see it here at the store. 50c

And She Wanted A Doll House

You will, too, when you see this adorable house. It is about 19 inches long, and very easy to put up. It is white with green trimmings and a red roof. The back is open so that you can put the furniture in. 1.00

Advertisement for a Trixytoy cardboard house from a "Toy-Town Circus" flyer issued by the J.F. Colson & Co. from St. Charles, Illinois, circa 1920s. The house sold for $1.00 and was white with green trim and a red roof. It was 19" wide.

Trixytoy living room furniture made by the Durrel firm, circa late 1920s. The furniture is 1/2" to one foot in scale and is made of four layers of cardboard that were glued together. See *Furnished Dollhouses 1880s-1980s* for photographs of the kitchen and dining room furniture ($30+). *Photograph and furniture from the collection of Evangeline Steinmeier.*

1930s

Something new!

Terre Town Playhouses

For Indoor and Outdoor Play

All Year Sales
Quick Turnover
Liberal Profits
Retail at Low Prices

Item No. 15 ..... Retails for 10c
Item No. 50 ..... Retails for 50c
Item No. 200 ..... Retails for $1.
Item No. 300 ..... Retails for $2.

See Terre Town Playhouse—Next Page

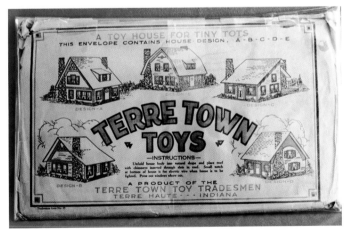

Envelope containing one of the small Terre Town Playhouses. Only one house is included in the package even though five are pictured on the front. These small #15 houses sold for 10 cents each. There was no back entry to the houses ($35-45). 8" high x 5 1/2" wide x 7 1/2" deep. *From the collection of Arliss and Gene Morris. Photograph by Gene Morris.*

Advertisement for Terre Town Playhouses made by Terre Town Toy Tradesmen of Terre Haute, Indiana. The ad appeared in *Toys and Novelties* in 1930. The houses came in several sizes. The smallest houses sold for only 10 cents. The largest house, No. 200, was 22" high x 20" wide x 15" deep. A large Indian Tepee was also available. All of the products were made of corrugated fibreboard (cardboard) and printed in bright colors.

Several cardboard dollhouses were advertised in the Montgomery Ward Christmas catalog for 1933. The prices ranged from 95 cents (with furniture) to $1.89. The house on the right was apparently made by the Toy and Novelty Division of the Androscoggin Pulp Co. of South Windham, Maine. *From the collection of Marge Meisinger.*

This cardboard "Mammoth Doll House" appears to be another version of the house in the Montgomery Ward Christmas catalog for 1933. This design has no sun room or garage. The "Directions for Assembly" credit the Toy and Novelty Division of the Androscoggin Pulp Co. in South Windham, Maine as the maker but the roof is marked "Wilmot Corp., South Windham." (unfurnished house $125+). 16 1/2" high x 21" wide x 13" deep. *House from the collection of Judith Mosholder. Photograph by Gary Mosholder.*

The inside of the "Mammoth" dollhouse has been furnished with four rooms of 3/4" Strombecker wood furniture. The four openings in the back allow access to the rooms. *Mosholder Collection.*

The cardboard Sutherland Play-Time Doll House No 200 was advertised in the Montgomery Ward Christmas catalog for 1933. The house was furnished with thirty-six pieces of wood Jaymar Happy Hour furniture and sold for $1.89 complete. *From the collection of Marge Meisinger.*

Play-Time cardboard Doll House No. 6, Set No. 11 made by the Warren Paper Products Co. in Lafayette, Indiana, circa mid 1930s. The base of the one-room cardboard house is made from the bottom of its box. The back of the house is open ($30). 8 1/4" high x 11" wide x 8" deep. *Photograph and house from the collection of Bonnie Benson Hanson.*

The five-room cardboard Play-Town house was manufactured by the Sutherland Paper Company in Kalamazoo, Michigan in the early 1930s. The house is pictured furnished with the wood Happy Hour pieces made by the Jaymar Specialty Co. located in New York. See *Antique and Collectible Dollhouses* for more photographs of the Happy Hour furniture (unfurnished house $100-125). 18" high x 13" wide x 12 1/2" deep. *Photograph and house from the collection of Patty Cooper.*

Four-room cardboard Play-Time Doll House No. 20, Set No. 14. made by the Warren Paper Products Co., circa mid 1930s. The outside of the house is printed with a brick pattern as well as shutters ($60-80). 13" high x 14" wide x 9 1/2" deep. *Photograph and house from the collection of Becky Norris.*

The inside of the four-room house has no decoration on its walls or floor. The back of the house is open for play. The original price tag of 20 cents can still be read on the box bottom, which becomes the base of the house when it is put together. *Norris Collection.*

Five-room cardboard Built-Rite Doll House, circa 1940s. The house is open in the back for play. It was advertised in *Children's Activities* magazine of November 1949 priced at $1.25 (MIB $60-80). 13" high x 20" wide x 11" deep. *From the collection of Arliss and Gene Morris. Photograph by Gene Morris.*

One-room cardboard Built-Rite Toy House (later trade name for Warren Paper Product toys), circa late 1930s. It is set No. 9 (MIB $50-60). *From the collection of Arliss and Gene Morris. Photograph by Gene Morris.*

Below:
Unusual boxed cardboard Built-Rite Toy Fence with a total length of eight feet. The pieces could be used for a fence around a dollhouse or as a Christmas tree fence ($50+). See earlier books for more information and photographs of Built-Rite products. *Fence from the collection of Judith Mosholder. Photograph by Gary Mosholder.*

1940s

Two cardboard furnished houses were advertised in the Sears 1940 Christmas catalog. The "Country Estate" came furnished with forty-five pieces of metal Tootsietoy furniture to be used in the living room, dining room, kitchen, two bedrooms, and a bathroom. It sold for $1.98 complete. The "Budget" house furniture was made of fiberboard and included sixty-three pieces to furnish seven rooms. It sold for 79 cents. It is thought that both houses were made by the O.B. Andrews Co., located in Chattanooga, Tennessee. *From the collection of Marge Meisinger.*

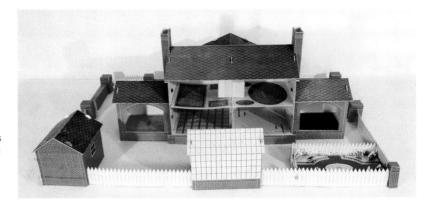

The back of the Andrews house is open to provide access to its six rooms. Rugs and other floor coverings are printed on the floors. The garden and greenhouse can be seen from this angle. *Private Collection.*

Cardboard "Country Estate" dollhouse as advertised in the Sears 1940 Christmas catalog. The bottom of the instruction sheet lists its maker as "O.B. Andrews Co." When assembled, the house included a garage, fence, garden and greenhouse ($125-150). House 16" high x 35 1/2" wide x 14 1/2" deep. *Private Collection.*

New Modern Home Doll House with Seven Rooms as advertised in the Sears 1940 Christmas catalog. This house, thought to have been made by the O.B. Andrews Company of Chattanooga, Tennessee, was to be assembled using a lock and tuck method. See *Antique and Collectible Dollhouses and Their Furnishings* for another example of an Andrews seven-room cardboard house ($60-80). *Courtesy of The Toy and Miniature Museum of Kansas City.*

Seven-room cardboard house as advertised in the Sears catalog in 1944. It was furnished with thirteen pieces of Nancy Forbes wood furniture and thirteen pieces of cardboard furniture (kitchen and porch). Although the house is entirely different than any known Andrews house, the design does carry out the theme of two wings with curved openings on the back side of the structure and it contains seven rooms as do two of the known Andrews houses. The house sold for $2.55 complete with furniture. *From the collection of Marge Meisinger.*

Cardboard house as advertised in the Sears catalog in 1944. The awnings on the front windows are missing. The house features seven rooms, sun decks, and a garage ($75+). 15 1/4" high x 31" wide x 12" deep. *Photograph and house from the collection of Marge Powell.*

The inside of the Sears seven-room house has space for a kitchen, dining room, living room, sun room, two bedrooms, and a bathroom. The walls and floors are printed with rugs, windows and curtains. Several pieces of Built-Rite cardboard furniture are shown in the house. *Powell Collection.*

Boxed Concord #132 cardboard dollhouse and #120 cardboard furniture, circa 1940. The Concord Toy Co. was located in New York City and manufactured several different styles of dollhouses. See *Antique and Collectible Dollhouses and Their Furnishings* for another example. (dollhouse MIB $100-125, furniture $60+). 12" high x 27 1/2" wide x 14 3/4" deep. *Photograph, house and furniture from the collection of Becky Norris.*

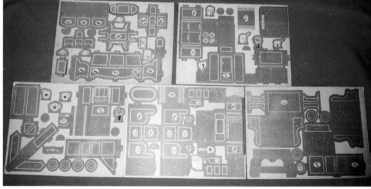

The Concord cardboard furniture included forty-eight pieces to furnish a living room, kitchen, bedroom, and dining room. *Norris Collection.*

The "Benda-Toy" house contains one room furnished with its original cardboard furniture. The inside walls are decorated. The roof is made using the house's box. *Norris Collection.*

"Benda-Toy" Dollhouse made by National Playthings in the U.S.A., circa early 1940s. The cardboard house is surrounded by a yard and fence. The front of the house has been painted silver (with repainted front $50-60). Base 18" wide x 10" deep, house 11 1/2" high x 13" wide x 8" deep. *Photograph and house from the collection of Becky Norris.*

The cardboard furniture is put together with metal hinges. Furniture includes a sofa, wing chair, table, chair, cabinet, and cradle. There is also a cardboard baby in the cradle. *Norris Collection.*

"Benda-Toy" furnished rooms were also produced by National Playthings. A living room, dining room, and bedroom were advertised in the N. Shure Co. catalog for 1941. The copy says they are new products and "the pieces are shaped by bending the metal joints." Each room came with figures that could be made to sit, stand, walk, or play. The walls of the rooms were hinged to the box. Each set included thirteen pieces to furnish that particular room. *From the collection of Marge Meisinger.*

"Benda-Toy" Doll Living Room. A new creation made of heavy fibre board, finished in colors. The pieces are shaped by bending. Have metal joints. Figures can be made to sit, stand, walk, run or play. Contains 13 pieces. Furnished with walls hinged to box.
No. 42N81. Per dozen sets. 8.00

"Benda-Toy" Doll Dining Room. Figures and furniture are made of fibre-board, and can be arranged in many positions because of metal joints. Nicely colored in washable finish. Complete set of 13-pieces in box, with colored walls furnished.
No. 42N83. Per dozen sets.... 8.00

"Benda-Toy" Doll Bed Roo Figures and furniture are made fibre-board, hinged, enabling the to be set up in many differe positions. Realistically colore Complete set of 12-pieces set i box with walls.
No. 42N82. Per dozen sets. 8.0

This circa late 1930s to early 1940s cardboard kitchen was issued to advertise the Florence Stove Co. of Gardner, Massachusetts. Besides the stove, other furniture included a tall cabinet, refrigerator (no coil on top), "built-in sink," and chair. Cabinets and floor covering are printed on the walls ($50). 6.5" high x 12" wide x 11" deep. *Photograph and room from the collection of Ruth Petros.*

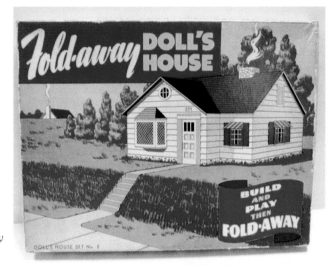

Box for unidentified cardboard "Fold-away Doll's House," circa 1940s. The only information on the box is set No 2. *From the collection of Judy Mosholder. Photographs by Gary Mosholder.*

The outside of the "Fold-away" house included an unusual front window along with an awning over its other window. The box bottom has been used as the base of the house. The inside contains only one room with no inside decoration ($35-45). 7 1/2" high x 13 1/2" wide x 10 1/4" deep. *Mosholder Collection.*

Unidentified chalet type cardboard house, circa 1946. The front opens and latches. The house includes one undecorated room, wood chimney, and tissue paper type window panes. A matching shed with two stalls was also produced. Collector Marge Powell received one of these houses for a childhood birthday in 1946 ($35+). 6 1/2" high x 6 1/2" wide x 8 1/2" deep. *From the collection of Arliss and Gene Morris. Photograph by Gene Morris.*

Cardboard "Let's Play House" produced by Game Makers Co. of Long Island City, New York. This circa 1940s six-room house could be completely assembled instantly. It was made to quickly fold flat for storage by removing the brads holding it together. The house was fully decorated on the inside ($35-45). 13 1/2" high x 19" wide x 8 1/2" deep.

Box for the cardboard Dixon Doll House manufactured by Jefferson, located in Philadelphia, Pennsylvania, circa late 1940s.

The Jefferson dollhouse contained four rooms with decorated floors only ($45). 14 1/2" high x 20" wide x 11 3/4" deep.

Four-room cardboard house produced by Jayline Manufacturing Co. Inc., circa mid to late 1940s. The company was located in Egg Harbor City, New Jersey. A small porch roof is missing on the left side of the house and the house also originally had a chimney. A fence was supplied for the right side of the house ($35 with missing parts). 14" high x 17" wide x 7 1/2" deep.

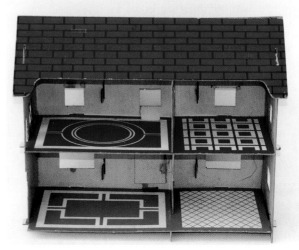

The inside of the Jayline house includes plain walls and decorated floors. Although the house is not marked, the original instruction sheet identified the house as a Jayline made product. See earlier books for more information and houses, including metal, made by Jayline.

Recent Cardboard Houses

Cardboard "La Maison Kleenex" house made to advertise Kleenex products ($35+). 15" high x 14 3/4" wide x 10" deep. *House from the collection of Arliss and Gene Morris. Photograph by Gene Morris.*

The inside of the Kleenex house contains seven rooms and a hall. The walls and floors are colorfully decorated. The house opens and closes like a suitcase. *Morris collection.*

A cardboard Waltons dollhouse was advertised in the Sears 1975 Christmas catalog. The house was a tie-in product to *The Waltons* television program, then showing on CBS. The series began in 1972 and ended its run in 1981. The house sold for $5.33.

The cardboard Walton Playset, made by Amsco, as advertised in the Sears 1975 catalog. The box bottom became the base of the house. Eleven figures and a truck came with the set (MIB $50-75). House 12 1/2" high x 19 1/2" wide x 13 1/2" deep. *Photograph and house from the collection of Bonnie Benson Hanson.*

The inside of the Walton house contained five rooms with colorful walls printed with furniture. A rocker, seesaw, and swing also came with the set. A larger cardboard Walton house was made by Mego also in 1975 (see *American Dollhouses and Furniture* for photographs of this house). *Hanson collection.*

"Pop-up Dollhouse" made by South Bend Toy Mfg. Co. Inc., A Milton Bradley Co., from South Bend Indiana in 1978. Three different designs of the house were produced, including a Colonial, Contemporary, and Victorian. *Photograph and house from the collection of Marge Powell.*

Each Pop-up dollhouse contains two rooms and a patio. The rooms include decorated walls and floors, as well as furniture printed on the walls. The Colonial and Contemporary models are pictured ($35+ each). 9" tall x 14 1/2" wide x 10" deep. *Powell Collection.*

Handmade Houses

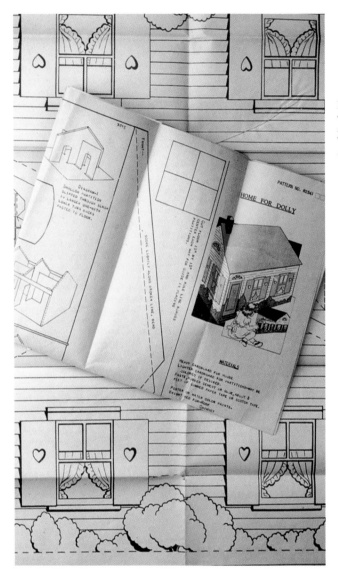

Home For Dolly Pattern #R2341. The paper pattern was to be painted, mounted on cardboard, cut out, and then assembled to make a 15" x 15" dollhouse. The pattern appears to be the type that could be ordered from a newspaper, circa early 1940s.

Dollhouse constructed recently using pattern #R2341. The original pattern was painted and mounted on poster board. The roof was also made of poster board using the pattern's measurements. 9.5" high x 15" wide x 15" deep. *House assembled by Jeff Zillner.*

The inside of the house contains four rooms, two on each side. The house can be accessed by opening the front or back sections. In order to photograph the inside of the house, the back section has been removed. These rooms have been decorated with watercolor paints. Wallpaper would also be appropriate. The house has been furnished with Jaymar wood furniture.

Handmade cardboard dollhouse that may have been produced from a cardboard box. Thin pieces of cardboard were added to the roof for shingles. All of the windows have applied pictures cut from magazines to indicate interior and exterior scenes. Window panes are made of cellophane. The sink is dated 1966 (not enough examples to determine price). 26" high x 18 1/4" wide x 7 3/4" deep. *Photograph and house from the collection of Bonnie Benson Hanson.*

The cardboard house contains six rooms and an attic, all furnished with handmade furniture and accessories. Balsa wood, pipe cleaners, paper, cardboard, matchsticks, beads, putty, and cloth were used to construct the furnishings. *Hanson Collection.*

Some of the many pieces of furniture for the homemade cardboard house include a sofa, chairs, lamps, piano, table, bed, clock and a rocking horse. *Hanson Collection.*

Chapter 3
American Dollhouses and Furniture

Although many American manufacturers of dollhouses and furniture have been featured in the previous books, new companies continue to come to light. New firms included in this chapter are Roger Williams Toys, Wicker Toy Mfg. Co., America Toy Co., Millnick Mfg. Co., and Mother Goose Toys. Additional examples from Rich, Keystone, Schoenhut, Tootsietoy, Converse, Jayline, Macris, and Wisconsin Toy as well as other firms are also pictured. The "Furnished Dollhouses" chapter also includes many more American houses and furnishings.

Unidentified Lithographed Houses

Unidentified, perhaps American, lithographed paper over wood dollhouse advertised in the Carl P. Stirn catalog in 1893. This house is unusual in that the lithography includes all the architectural details on the front of the house. Included are the window, door, awning type porch roof, porch, steps, sidewalk, yard, and even a little girl sitting on the porch. A similar house was also made in a larger size. The houses had open backs and appear to be two stories tall on the outside but each contained only one room. Both houses were advertised in the Stirn catalog and the copy stated that the houses could be used as one house or two ($500 with missing paper). 11" high x 8" wide x 4" deep. The larger house measured 16" high x 8.75" wide x 7" deep. The smaller house could fit inside the larger model for storage. *Photograph and house from the collection of Marge Powell.*

Stirn and Lyon

The Stirn & Lyon firm, located in New York, first patented their dollhouses in 1881. The houses came in wood boxes and the consumer was expected to assemble the pieces into a dollhouse. This was no easy task. The box was to be used as the base of the house. The house was made of thin wood that was to be constructed using the provided dowels and pegs. The finished houses were not very sturdy or stable. Perhaps that is why these houses still end up in their original boxes—they were used very little. This Stirn & Lyon box is labeled "Combination/Doll House/Patented 1881/by Stirn & Lyon/New York." The same company also made a larger "Combination Doll Mansion" house (MIB $1,000+). 22.5" high x 18" wide x 9.75" deep. *Photograph and house from the collection of Evangeline Steinmeier.*

The inside of the house features lithography similar to that used in the Dunham's Cocoanut house, circa 1890s. Like the Dunham's house, furniture, fireplace, cabinets, accessories, and wall and floor coverings are all printed on the lithographed paper. The decorative piece under the roof is exactly like that used on the larger house. Even the two chimney shadows appear on the roof papers. *Powell Collection.*

Unidentified lithographed paper over wood house, perhaps American, circa early 1900s. The small brightly colored house has an opening front door but the windows and other architectural details are done with lithographed paper. The entry overhang provides a second floor balcony supported by turned columns ($650-750). 12" high x 9.5" wide x 6" deep. *Photograph and house from the collection of Linda Boltrek.*

Bliss

Lithographed paper over wood house very similar to the Bliss No. 202 house featured in the 1911 Bliss catalog (firm located in Pawtucket, Rhode Island). This house has several differences from the houses more easily found by collectors that features the "R. Bliss Co." name above the porch roof. This model does not have a second floor balcony extending across its front, has no downstairs porch railings, has printed instead of metal balcony railing, and is decorated with only one piece of wood trim above the upstairs windows instead of the more usual two. Therefore, it is hard to date this house ($1,200-1,500). 17" high x 11.5" wide x 8" deep. *Photograph and house from the collection of Leslie and Joanne Payne.*

The inside of the small lithographed house contains two rooms which could be furnished with the small scale metal furniture made in Germany or France or the Adrian Cooke "pewter" pieces made in Chicago. *Boltrek Collection.*

The inside of the unusual lithographed paper over wood house raises even more questions. The back walls of the two rooms are papered with designs used on original boxes for one of Bliss's other toys. Was the Bliss company using papers and pieces that were available in order to allow them to produce houses more cheaply or did another firm market the house after Bliss was sold in 1914? The mystery remains. *Payne Collection.*

Peter Pia

Cardboard room like the one shown in a 1900 Montgomery Ward advertisement as pictured by Flora Gill Jacobs in her book *Dolls' Houses in America*. The Montgomery Ward parlor was furnished with a wood table (see kitchen), four chairs, mirror over the fireplace, and an easel complete with a picture. The Montgomery Ward furnished room sold for 25 cents. The lightweight metal furniture, with cardboard seats, is similar to that made by Adrian Cooke of Chicago but has been attributed to Peter Pia, a New York firm. The walls and floors of the room were printed with wall coverings, pictures and floor coverings. The outside walls were imitation brick. The table and birdcage are not original to the room. See *Antique and Collectible Dollhouses* for more information ($295 furnished). 9" high x 11" wide x 9.5" deep. *Photograph and room from the collection of Patty Cooper.*

The "Peter Pia" kitchen is decorated with "wainscoting" along with pictures, a clock, windows, and floor covering. The table and chairs are original to the room while the stove and sideboard are additions. The original furniture for the kitchen included a range plus the table and two chairs pictured ($295 furnished). 9" high x 11" wide x 9.5" deep. *Photograph and room from the collection of Patty Cooper..*

Roger Williams Toys

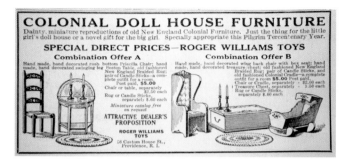

Roger Williams Toys advertisement from *Good Housekeeping* magazine of November 1921. The firm was located in Providence, Rhode Island where they made "New England Colonial" dollhouse furniture similar to Tynietoy. The furniture was priced from $1.50 to $2.50 for each piece or could be purchased in a group setting for $5.00. The ad stated that the furniture was "Just the thing for the little girl's doll house." *From the collection of Leslie and Joanne Payne.*

Roger Williams settee and matching Priscilla chairs with rush seats and hand painted decorations. The furniture is slightly larger than 1" to one foot in scale. The furniture was marked with a sticker or a stamp which read "A Roger Williams Toy." *Payne Collection.*

Roger Williams bed, tilt-top tables, and chest. Some accessories were also sold with the furniture. Included were candle sticks and small braided rugs (not enough examples to determine price). *Payne Collection.*

This canopy bed and grandfather clock were also Roger Williams products. Both feature hand painted decorations. The bed is missing its canopy (not enough examples to determine price). *Payne Collection.*

Tootsietoy

Tootsietoy advertisement which appeared in the Butler Brothers catalog for October 1929. The small 1/2" to one foot scaled metal furniture was made by the Dowst Brothers Co., located in Chicago, beginning in the early 1920s. Besides furniture, cardboard houses were also marketed by the firm to be used with the furniture. The houses may have been produced by the Wayne Paper Products firm. Pictured in this advertisement is the early line of Tootsietoy furniture and one of the cardboard houses. *From the collection of Marge Meisinger.*

This cardboard six-room house is marked on the inside "No 12/Tootsietoy/ Doll House." These houses usually had some type of decoration on the inside walls and floors. The chimney on this house is missing ($350). 22" high x 23" wide. *Photograph and house from the collection of Linda Boltrek.*

Set of boxed Tootsietoy metal kitchen furniture using the same box pictured in the Butler Brothers advertisement. The early kitchen set did not include moving parts. See earlier books for more information and photographs of the Tootsietoy products ($150-200). *Photograph and furniture from the collection of Marilyn Pittman.*

A full page ad in color appeared in the December 1930 *Child Life* magazine to promote the new line of Tootsietoy furniture and the Mansion. This new metal furniture retained the small scale of the earlier pieces but the new designs were made more up-to-date and included moving parts. The furniture was priced at $1.00 for each room. The cardboard Mansion with a Spanish look sold for $5.00 unfurnished or $10.00 complete with furniture.

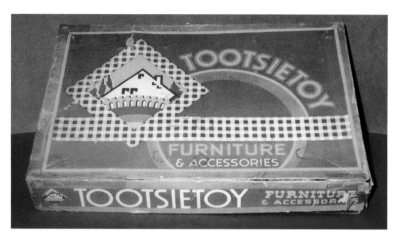

In the 1930s, Tootsietoy began offering boxed sets of furniture that were accompanied by appropriate accessories. These boxes included the later 1930s sets of furniture. This is one of the boxes that once held these products (box only $20-30). *Photograph and box from the collection of Marilyn Pittman.*

Dowst Brothers also used the trade names "Daisy" and "My Dolly's Furniture" to market the Tootsietoy metal furniture. Sears carried a "Daisy" line in 1928 and some of the cardboard houses were also marked with the "Daisy" trademark (box only $20-30). *Pittman Collection.*

Metal furniture was also produced in France, which apparently used the patterns from the early line of the Tootsietoy furniture. Pictured are dining room and living room pieces. Each item is marked "FRANCE" ($10-20 each). *Photograph and furniture from the collection of Evangeline Steinmeier.*

Schoenhut

Schoenhut dollhouse made of "Wood and fibreboard, embossed to represent stone walls and tile roofs." The A. Schoenhut Co. was located in Philadelphia, Pennsylvania and manufactured both dollhouses and wood furniture for several years in the 1920s and 1930s (see earlier books for more information and photographs of these products). This house was featured in the Schoenhut catalog in 1923. Several different models of these houses were produced, including one-story bungalows. This design contains five rooms plus an attic, which can be accessed when the roof is removed ($2,000+). 24" high x 16" wide x 22.5" deep. *Photograph and house from the collection of Bonnie Benson Hanson.*

The inside rooms are covered with lithographed paper to represent wall coverings and doors. Both sides of the house open to allow access to the five rooms. The opened right side is pictured. *Bonnie Benson Hanson Collection.*

Schoenhut house with a printed red brick finish. It is pictured in the firm's catalog for 1933 and 1934. The house contains four rooms and came with a staircase and electric lights. The attic is not accessible. The back is removable to allow access to the rooms ($1,200+). 24.5" high x 26" wide x 17.75" deep. *Photograph and house from the collection of Patty Cooper.*

Mother Goose Toys

Additional pieces of "Mother Goose Toys" furniture. The doors are functional on the dresser and the desk. The light colored bed may be the crib to the nursery. *Bonnie Benson Hanson Collection.*

Set of 1" to one foot scaled wood dollhouse dining room furniture labeled "Mother Goose Toys," circa mid to late 1920s. The pieces were made by Mary Harison Phinizy Fox in Augusta, Georgia. She began making furniture as a hobby, using scraps of cigar box wood, in the mid-1920s. The furniture attracted enough interest that the production grew into a cottage industry. The well-known toy store F.A.O. Schwarz purchased some of the furniture and perhaps dollhouses from the firm. Mary Phinizy even shared at least one dollhouse that was featured in the Schwarz Christmas window. Phinizy married Dr. William Fox, circa 1932, and moved to Atlantic City, New Jersey. Apparently, the Mother Goose Toys firm ended about that time after a period of approximately six years in business (not enough examples to determine price). *Photograph and furniture from the collection of Bonnie Benson Hanson.*

Mother Goose 1" to one foot scale nursery furniture, circa late 1920s. Included are a three drawer chest, table, rocking chair, playpen, table lamp, clothes hanger, and shoofly rocker (not enough examples to determine price). *Photograph and furniture from the collection of Patty Cooper.*

Two pieces of Mother Goose furniture showing the original printed labels. They read "Mother Goose Toys/Patent applied for/2223 Kings Way/ Augusta, Georgia." It is not known if the items sold by F.A.O. Schwarz included the Mother Goose markings or if the store added their own labels. *Photograph and furniture from the collection of Bonnie Benson Hanson.*

Wicker Toy Mfg. Co.

Wicker Toy Mfg. Co. advertisement in *Toys and Novelties* magazine for February 1930. The copy from the Columbus, Ohio firm says the line of furniture included "Sufficient numbers to completely furnish the modern doll house with Wicker, Overstuffed, Chintz Bedroom, etc." The firm was to be at the Toy Fair with Macris Co. (maker of Dolly Ann Doll Houses) of Toledo, Ohio.

Wicker dollhouse furniture probably made by the Wicker Toy Mfg. Co. of Columbus, Ohio in the 1930s. The plant stand looks exactly like the one pictured in the "Wicker" ad from 1930. The furniture is 1" to one foot in scale and came with cushions (set $100-125). *Photograph and furniture from the collection of Gail and Ray Carey.*

Wisconsin Toy Co.

Living room sofa, rocking chair, and radio made by the Wisconsin Toy Co. of Milwaukee, Wisconsin, circa 1930s. The furniture is a large 1" to one foot in scale and the sofa is stamped "Goldilocks." Other Wisconsin Toy furniture is sometimes marked "Wis/Toy/Co." in a triangle. This overstuffed sofa and chair are pictured in the company catalog with another chair without rockers and a Davenport table and end table. The five piece living room set sold for $5.00 ($100-125 for three pieces).

This Wisconsin Toy "Bedroom Suite" was shown in the company catalog along with a chair, rocking chair, and three drawer chest. The folding screen had to be purchased separately for 50 cents. The furniture was decorated with decals (set $125-140). *Photograph and furniture from the collection of Evangeline Steinmeier.*

Love Seat Set E. M. 2

Sewed into a gift box $3.50

7-piece living room set of comfortable Art Moderne design. Finished in the popular light mahogany. Seats and back upholstered with brocade.

31—Love Seat ....$ .60
32—High back chair ... .50
33—Low back chair ... .50
35—Clock .... .45
40—End table 2*
41—Davenport table ... .50
42—Book shelf .... .50

Extra Item

57—Radio .... .50

58 Corner Cabinet 60

Goldilock's
LOVE SEAT SET

The Wisconsin Toy radio was shown in the catalog with a set of furniture called "Love Seat Set." Each piece of furniture could also be purchased separately. The radio was priced at 50 cents. *From the collection of Leslie and Joanne Payne.*

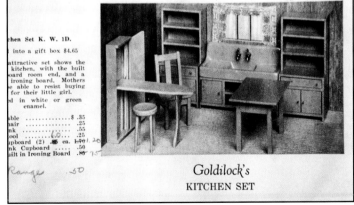

chen Set K. W. 1D.

into a gift box $4.65

attractive set shows the kitchen, with the built oard room end, and a ironing board. Mothers e able to resist buying for their little girl.

d in white or green enamel.

able ....$ .35
hair .... .25
nk .... .55
ool .... .25
pboard (2) .45 ea. 1.70
nk Cupboard ..... .50
ilt in Ironing Board .85

Range .50

Goldilock's
KITCHEN SET

One of the kitchen sets pictured in the Wisconsin Toy catalog from the 1930s. At least three different models of sinks are known to have been made. This kitchen shows the sink that sits on a base. *From the collection of Leslie and Joanne Payne.*

This sink (missing its faucets) is the same one pictured in the catalog. It is pictured with an ice box from the same firm. The doors and drawers on Wisconsin Toy furniture are functional. The sink originally sold for 55 cents ($75 for two pieces). *Photograph and furniture from the collection of Gail and Ray Carey.*

America Toy Co.

Enameled wood bedroom furniture, circa 1930s. The large furniture is approximately 1 1/4" - 1 1/2" to one foot in scale. Most of the furniture is quite "chunky" in design except for the chairs and rocker, which have a much more dainty look. The doors and the drawers are functional. All of the pieces are decorated with decals (set $75-100). *Furniture from the collection of Mary Lu Trowbridge. Photograph by Bob Trowbridge.*

The bottom of the furniture carries a label that reads "Toy/Company/America's Santa Claus/America." *Photograph by Bob Trowbridge.*

Lincoln Furniture

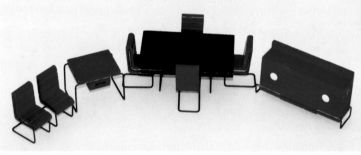

Lincoln Art Deco styled dining room furniture in 3/4" to one foot scale, circa 1936. The pieces were made by J.L. Wright, Inc., based in Chicago. Four rooms of the furniture were produced (see *Antique and Collectible Dollhouses* for more examples). They included a kitchen and living room. The dining room set originally consisted of ten pieces. Besides a table, six chairs, sideboard and serving pieces, a lamp was probably included in the set. The Lincoln furniture was made of wood and steel wire to reflect the Art Deco style then popular (set $135-150).

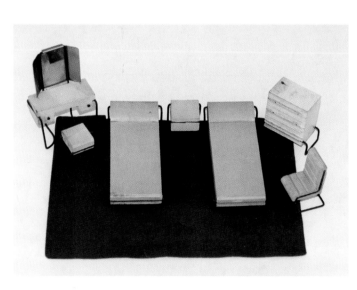

The Lincoln bedroom furniture consisted of nine pieces. Besides the two beds, dresser, vanity and bench, night stand and chair, a table lamp and floor lamp were also part of the original set. The furniture was advertised in the Butler Brothers catalog in 1936 and also in *Child Life* magazine in 1936. Besides the sets already mentioned, a sun room was also available. Each set sold for $1.00 (set $110+).

Rich Toy Co.

Early Rich house, circa mid 1930s. These houses were produced by the Rich Toy Manufacturing Co. in Clinton, Iowa. The early houses were made of wood and Gypsum board and featured metal strips across the top of the roof and on the corners for extra support. This house has paper shutters, flower boxes, and lanterns on either side of the front door for added decoration. The trees also appear to be original. The house contains six rooms and was wired for electricity. The back of the house is open to allow access to its rooms. Since no interior decoration was used, the inside of the house is unfinished dark brown ($150-200). 19.5" high (including chimney), 31" wide x 17" deep. *Photograph and house from the collection of Roy Specht.*

Rich two-room house, circa 1930s. The house has the metal reinforcements on the roof and corners, paper shutters, and original acetate windows. The lanterns, trees, and flowers are printed on the front of the house. The open backed house includes two rooms ($75-100). 9" high x 15.5" wide x 9" deep. *Photograph and house from the collection of Marge Powell.*

Another very similar small two-room Rich house, also from the 1930s. This house has a deck, to be accessed through the side door. The deck is made with a trellis-like covering supported by posts ($100-125). 9" high x 22.5" wide x 9" deep. *Powell Collection.*

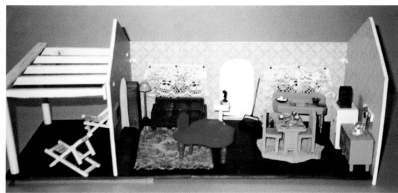

The inside of the Rich "trellis" house contains one large room and the deck-porch. The roof lifts off to allow easier access to the open backed house. The inside of the house was originally unfinished brown. The current owner has added wallpaper to give the house needed color. It has been furnished with 3/4" to one foot Strombecker wood furniture from the 1930s. *Powell Collection.*

Rich Colonial six-room house, circa mid 1930s. The house includes metal reinforcements, paper shutters, and flower boxes below the lower story windows. The covered entry porch is similar to one used in later years on some examples of Hall's Lifetime Toys houses ($150-175). 18" high to top of chimney x 31" wide x 12" deep plus 4.5" for the porch. *Photograph and house from the collection of Becky Norris.*

Rich Tudor house, also circa mid 1930s. It, too, has the metal pieces across the roof and on the corners. Flower boxes, paper shutters, and an interesting chimney add architectural interest. Unlike most Rich houses, this one has an added side door. The inside of the house has four rooms with plain brown walls. There is a lift-off roof in back to allow easy access to the upstairs. The house has an open back, as do nearly all of the Rich houses ($125+). 15.5" high x 23.25" wide x 9.5" deep. *Photograph and house from the collection of Becky Norris.*

Rich late 1930s house complete with a garage. Since not too many of the Rich houses featured garages, these houses are very much in demand. The original base on the house has been replaced. The inside of the back-opening house contains four rooms with unfinished brown walls and floors ($125). 16" high x 30.5" wide x 10" deep. *Photograph and house from the collection of Rita Goranson.*

This "Avon" three-room cottage was advertised in 1938. It was one of three Rich houses pictured in the All-American Products Corp. Christmas catalog for that year. The wholesale price was $1.47 with a retail price of $2.25. The ad stated that the house was made with pressed hardboard construction. The outside included metal on the corners as in the earlier years. The inside of the house was unfinished brown ($100+). 17.5" high x 22.35" wide x 9.75" deep. *Photograph and house from the collection of Evangeline Steinmeier.*

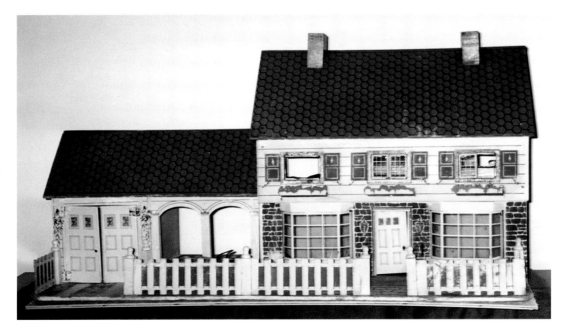

Unusual Rich house with a garage, breezeway, and fenced yard, circa late 1950s. The house also featured a doorbell. Like several of the Rich houses from the period, this one has two rounded picture windows on the front. Several of the opening windows are missing on the second story ($200+). 21" high with a base 40" wide x 17.5" deep. *Photograph and house from the collection of Rita Goranson.*

The inside of the Rich "Breezeway" house includes four rooms and the large breezeway featuring the usual Rich diamond floor pattern. *Goranson Collection.*

Rich house, circa late 1950s. Unlike most Rich houses, this one uses dark red and brown for its decor. The front of the base has been finished with a fuzzy green to simulate grass. The inside of the open backed house contains four rooms. Both the kitchen and bathroom floors are decorated with the familiar diamond tile pattern ($75+). 14" high x 22.5" wide x 10" deep. *House from the collection of Arliss and Gene Morris. Photograph by Gene Morris.*

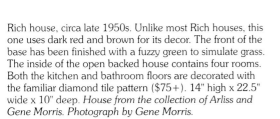

Montgomery Ward House

Advertisement in the Montgomery Ward Christmas catalog in 1945 for a plywood dollhouse. The copy read that the house was made from surplus pieces of material that had been used in government housing (World War II shortages still existed). It was called a "preview of the house of tomorrow." The house was interlocking so it could be set up or taken down in just a few minutes. No screws or nails were used. The open backed three-room house came with cellophane windows. The furniture pictured in the house was the newer Nancy Forbes line. It sold for $6.19 unfurnished. 11" high x 34" wide x 15.5" deep.

House pictured in the 1945 Montgomery Ward catalog. The 1950s car in front of the house is from a later period ($200+).*Photograph and house from the collection of George Mundorf.*

The inside of the three-room house has been furnished with an assortment of later "modern" pieces of furniture. The raised roof over the living room is very unusual architecture for a dollhouse of the period. *Mundorf Collection.*

Keystone Mfg. Co.

Masonite house, circa early 1940s, produced by the Keystone Mfg. Co. of Boston, Massachusetts. This same style house was also made with a two story addition (pictured in the firm's 1942-43 catalog) as well as with no addition at all. The house is missing flowers from its flower box and one awning. The open backed house contains five rooms. The inside of the house is not decorated as most of the later houses were. Instead, the walls and floors are plain brown. An electric fireplace came with the house ($150-175). 20" high (not including chimney) x 31" wide x 12" deep. *Photograph and house from the collection of Becky Norris.*

Keystone house, circa early 1940s, featuring metal casement windows, awnings (one missing) and unusual extra pieces connected to either side of the front step. The open backed house includes four rooms with plain brown walls and floors ($125+). 16" high (not including chimney) x 24" wide x 9.75" deep. *Norris Collection.*

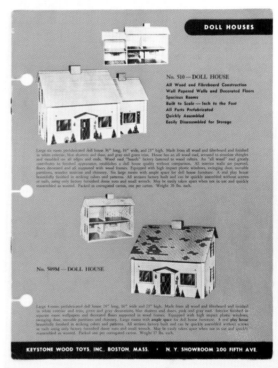

Keystone house pictured in the company catalog for 1955. The houses were made with wood and fibreboard construction. Like most of the later Keystone products, the houses featured decorated walls and floors. The house pictured at the bottom right contained four rooms and measured 23" high x 24" wide x 16" deep. *From the collection of Linda Boltrek.*

Large Keystone house pictured at the top of the page in the company catalog for 1955. The six-room house came with plastic windows, movable partitions, and a wood stairway. This house is finished in a light tan instead of white as the catalog describes. This model of the Keystone house includes a base, while no base is pictured in the Keystone catalog ($175-200). 23" high x 36" wide x 16" deep (base 1.5" high x 48" wide x 24" deep). *Photograph and house from the collection of Evangeline Steinmeier.*

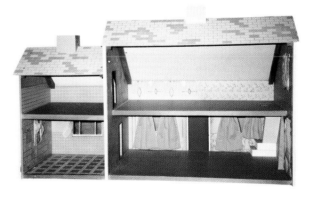

The inside of the circa 1955 Keystone house was finished with decorated walls and floors. The stairway can be seen in the right hand corner. If this house originally had movable partitions, they are missing. They were to be used to separate the two large rooms according to the owner's wishes. *Steinmeier Collection.*

Donna Lee

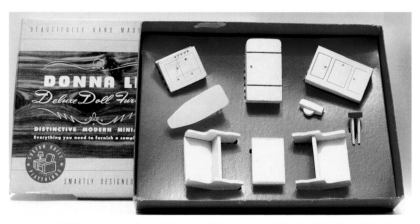

Boxed set of 3/4" to one foot Donna Lee wood furniture made by the Woodburn Manufacturing Co. in Chicago, circa 1940s. This boxed kitchen set appears to be a later issue than the more common furniture sold in the blue and pink boxes. The earlier kitchen table and chairs have been replaced by an attractive breakfast nook (boxed set $65-75). *Photograph and furniture from the collection of Patty Cooper.*

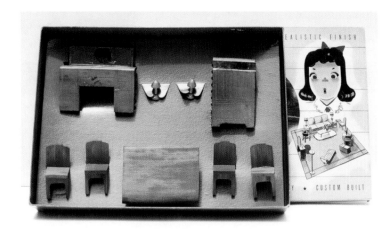

The Donna Lee wood dining room furniture in the gold box has also been improved. The set includes two lamps and restyled table, chairs, sideboard and cabinet (boxed set $65-75). *Cooper Collection.*

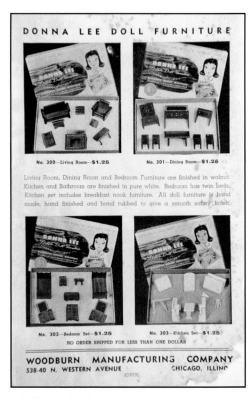

This flyer for the Donna Lee furniture pictures the living room, dining room, bedroom, and kitchen pieces that came in the gold and brown boxes. The sets sold for $1.25 each. All of the furniture is more attractive than the pieces that came in the pink and blue boxes.

Futurland Miniatures

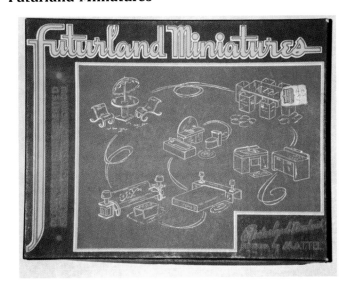

The "Futurland Miniatures" #506 box contains two lounge chairs and footstools plus a table with an umbrella. All pieces are 3/4" to one foot in scale. The original price tag reads $1.50 (boxed set $75). *Norris Collection*.

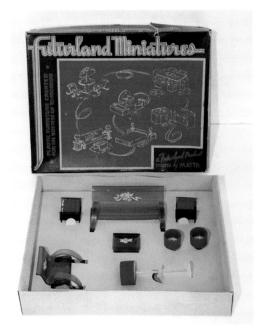

Boxed "Futurland Miniatures" marketed by Mattel Creations of Los Angeles, circa mid to late 1940s. The Plexiglas furniture came in several scales. This box pictures the 3/4" to one foot scale (see *Antique and Collectible Dollhouses* for other photographs of Mattel Creations products). This line of furniture may have been made a little later than the Mattel Twink-L-Toy furniture, which dates from 1945. The pictures on the Futurland Miniatures box show pieces for the living room, bedroom, kitchen, bathroom, dining room, and patio. The printing on the box reads "Plastic Furniture for the Hostess of Tomorrow." *Photograph and furniture from the collection of Becky Norris.*

Mattel "Futurland Miniatures" boxed living room furniture in 3/4" to one foot scale. Included are a sofa, chair, end table, coffee table, two table lamps, and a floor lamp. The plastic pieces are decorated with decals (boxed set $75). *Furniture from the collection of Marcie Tubbs. Photograph by Bob Tubbs.*

Renwal Manufacturing Co.

Black Renwal hard plastic furniture was produced by the Renwal Manufacturing Co. of Mineola, Long Island, N.Y. to be used as premiums by Cross and Blackwell Foods. This advertisement promoting the premiums appeared in *Better Homes and Gardens* magazine for February 1955. The ad stated the furniture was hand painted and could be purchased for 35 cents plus one label from any of the company's date, nut, chocolate, or fruit rolls. The furniture was advertised as "Pennsylvania Dutch Miniatures."

Included in the premium furniture pieces were a cupboard, rocker, server, dining room table, folding chairs and card table, dining chair, coffee table, cradle, lamp table, and highboy. Although the fireplace and potty chair were not included in the list, they may have been added later ($5-20 each). *Photograph and furniture from the collection of Roy Specht.*

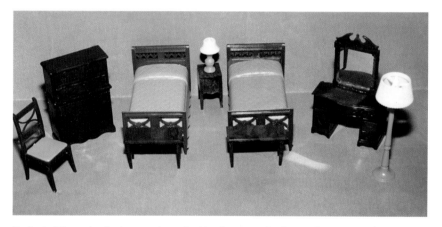

Dedicated Renwal collectors are always looking for unusual color combinations in the furniture. These bedroom pieces, which feature aqua bedspreads and lamps, are included in one of those hard-to-find sets (set $75). *Specht Collection.*

Although the Renwal firm discontinued the making of the plastic furniture in the early 1960s, furniture made with the Renwal molds continues to surface. This plastic dining room furniture is marked "Made in Hong Kong" (set $35-45). *Specht Collection.*

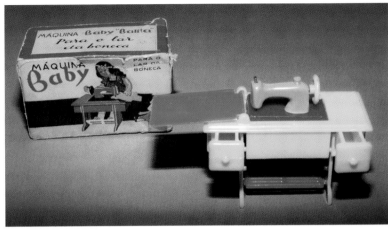

Boxed plastic sewing machine also made from the original Renwal design. The drawers are functional. This toy was made in Brazil (boxed $35). *Specht Collection.*

This packaged brown plastic dining room furniture, circa 1970s, also used the early Renwal design. The package is marked "Made in Hong Kong for Famous Corporation Brooklyn, New York" (packaged $35). *Specht Collection.*

Plasco

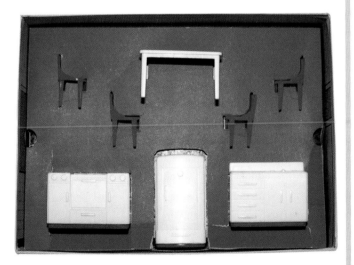

Hard plastic kitchen furniture made by the Plastic Art Toy Corp., located in East Paterson, N.J., circa late 1940s. This set is unusual because the chairs are red instead of the more usual blue ($75+). See earlier books for photographs and information on more Plasco products. *Specht Collection.*

Plastic one-story house, thought to be a Plasco product, circa early 1960s. The open backed house is made of plastic with a softer plastic roof ($150 furnished). 11" high to top of chimney x 33" wide x 13" deep. *Photograph and house from the collection of Roy Specht.*

The inside of the house is furnished with its original Plasco furniture. This later line from the early 1960s was modified somewhat, apparently to make the pieces cheaper to produce. The bottoms of the living room chairs, sofas, beds, etc. were eliminated, which gave these pieces a cheaper look. The house was furnished as a kitchen, dining room, living room, bathroom, and bedroom (a partition may be missing between the bathroom and bedroom). *Specht Collection.*

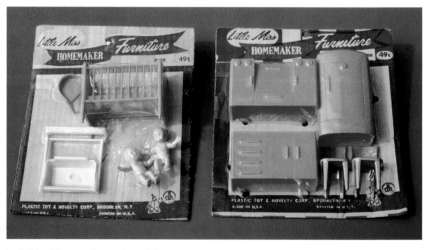

Little Miss Homemaker packaged furniture, which sold for 49 cents for each card. These were later products but each piece carried the Plasco mark. The company is listed as the Plastic Toy & Novelty Corp. in Brooklyn, New York. It is not known if the original Plasco firm was still producing this product ($45 each card). *Specht Collection.*

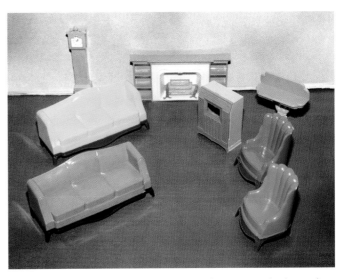

Boxed plastic furniture made with the Plasco molds. The box information reads "Plasco/Doll House/Furniture/REL Manufacturing Corp. East Patterson, N.J." The name changes and the shortcuts used in producing the furniture (no bottom on chair) indicates that changes had been made in the company but the original Plasco trade name was still included on the package ($45+). *From the collection of Marcie Tubbs. Photograph by Bob Tubbs.*

Unusual Plasco furniture, circa late 1960s, that features pastel colors in the furniture line. Although the Plasco name and the Little Drummer Boy trademark remain, "Made in U.S.A." has been scratched off. The furniture was evidently made in a foreign country. The original bottoms of the sofas and chairs are included on this line of furniture and the plastic used to made these pieces is a little softer than the original ($5-10 each piece). *Specht Collection.*

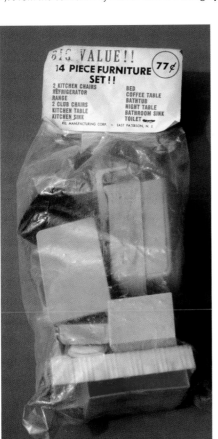

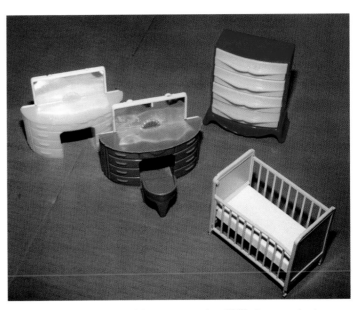

Additional pieces of "Plasco" furniture, circa late 1960s, in unusual colors. Until this furniture is found in an original box, it is difficult to know if it was still being sold as a Plasco product ($5-10 each). *Specht Collection.*

This package of furniture is also marked "REL Manufacturing Corp. East Patterson, New Jersey." Fourteen pieces of plastic furniture made from the Plasco molds sold in the package for only 77 cents ($35-45). *Specht Collection.*

Outdoor Plasco furniture was also made in pastel colors in later years. Even though the pieces were marked with the Plasco name, their date of production is unknown ($5-10 each). *Specht Collection.*

This set of plastic bathroom furniture was also based on the original Plasco molds but the package is marked "Arista Finest Quality Toys New York" ($20+). *Specht Collection.*

Like other plastic furniture molds, Plasco's designs have been used by other companies. This kitchen set with added opening doors looks exactly like the kitchen set made by Plasco (see page 160 in the *American Dollhouses and Furniture* book). This furniture is marked "Australia Marquis." All of the Plasco furniture in the various styles is in the 3/4" to one foot scale (not enough examples to determine price). *Specht Collection.*

Playwood Plastics Co. Inc.

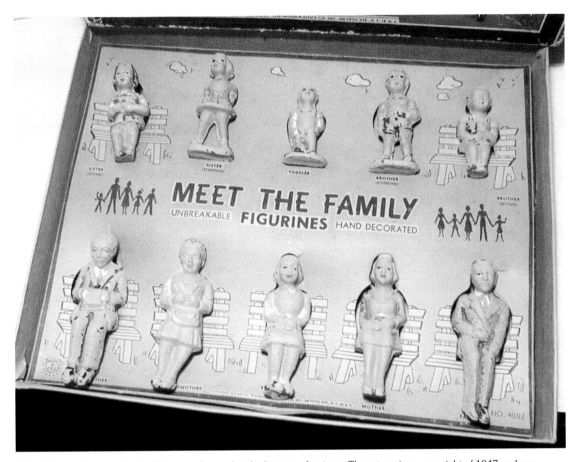

"Meet The Family" boxed set of figures to be used with plastic toy furniture. The set carries a copyright of 1947 and was made by Playwood Plastics Co. Inc., 200 Fifth Ave., New York 10, N.Y. The standing sister measures 3.75" tall. Ten figures were included, made in both standing and sitting positions. The box lid stated the "family was scaled to plastic toy furniture" (boxed $50+). *From the collection of Judith Mosholder. Photograph by Gary Mosholder.*

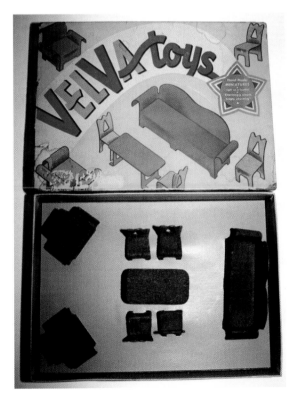

Velva Toys

Velva Toys boxed 3/4" to one foot living room furniture, circa late 1940s. The furniture was made of metal, which was then covered with a substance to give the surface a velvet feel. The added material appears heavier than the flocking added to other dollhouse furniture from the 1930s and 1940s. The furniture was made by the Millnick Mfg. Co., 315 N. Water St., Wichita 2, Kansas. The information on the box states that the contents are "Handmade Miniatures." The set includes a sofa, two easy chairs, a table, and four matching chairs. The box top pictures the same pieces of furniture (boxed $65+). *Photograph and furniture from the collection of Gail and Ray Carey.*

Louis Marx

Louis Marx & Co., headquartered in New York City, produced this unusual "Newlywed Room" with furniture, circa late 1950s or early 1960s. Marx metal Newlywed rooms had first been marketed by the firm in the 1920s. These tiny rooms were furnished with metal pieces approximately 1/4" to one foot in scale. The new rooms were also made of metal but they were furnished with the firm's regular 3/4" to one foot scale softer plastic furniture. Rooms were made for a living room, dining room, kitchen, bedroom, nursery, and bathroom (MIB each room $300). *Photograph and rooms from the collection of Evangeline Steinmeier.*

The Newlywed kitchen, nursery, and bathroom are made using the same room — just the furniture is different. *Steinmeier Collection.*

Marx Newlywed living room. The insides of the metal rooms were decorated with pictures, windows, floor, and wall coverings. The plastic furniture is the same as that used in the larger Marx metal houses of the period. It is 3/4" to one foot in scale. The current owner purchased all of these rooms in their original boxes from one individual (MIB $300 each room). 5.75" high x 9.5" wide x 9.5" deep. *Steinmeier Collection.*

The basic metal room used for the living room, dining room, and bedroom is also identical. The furniture included in the package identified the individual rooms. *Steinmeier Collection.*

Marx Newlywed dining room with all its original furniture. These rooms include only two walls instead of the more usual three usually included in room settings. *Steinmeier Collection.*

Marx Newlywed nursery, which included two children sitting in its furniture. *Steinmeier Collection.*

Marx plastic bathroom furniture, which came in the boxed Newlywed bathroom. This set of rooms appears to be very rare. *Steinmeier Collection.*

Marx plastic bedroom furniture and chair with added company decals. *Morris Collection.*

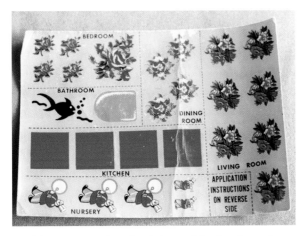

The Louis Marx company also offered sheets of decals to be used as decorations with their furniture. The instruction sheet (on the back of the decals) gave suggestions on where the decals should be placed in order to provide the most pleasing result. *From the collection of Arliss and Gene Morris. Photograph by Gene Morris.*

Although the metal Louis Marx houses were sold furnished, the firm also marketed individual rooms of furniture. Perhaps these were to be used as replacements or to furnish houses from other firms that were sold unfurnished. This 3/4" to one foot scale kitchen set, circa late 1950s or early 1960s, is made of the softer plastic used by the firm in the later years (mint card $45). *Photograph and furniture from the collection of Roy Specht.*

Marx 3/4" to one foot scaled living room and dining room furniture with Marx decals added for decoration. *Morris Collection.*

Marx 3/4" to one foot living room furniture on its original card, circa late
1950s or early 1960s. The furniture is the later softer plastic (mint card $45).
Specht Collection.

Marx 3/4" to one foot scale soft plastic bathroom furniture on its original
card. The mother and baby figures are also included (mint card $45). *Specht
Collection.*

Marx "Doll House Family" still on its original card,
circa late 1950s, early 1960s. Besides the plastic
adult and children figures, a dog is also part of the
set (mint card $35+). *Specht Collection.*

"Fantasy Doll House," circa 1971, the last metal house made by the Louis Marx Co. The house was called "A Take-a-long toy" because it came with a handle so it could be carried easily. The picture on the box shows the furniture that came with the house. The pieces included holes into which the peg-like dolls could be inserted. The house included two plastic windows plus a plastic door and chimney. It originally sold for $4.99 complete with furniture (MIB $100). *From the collection of Marcie Tubbs. Photograph by Bob Tubbs.*

Allied Molding Corp.

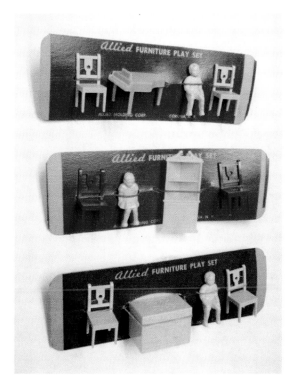

Allied 1/2" to one foot scale plastic furniture on original cards, circa 1950s. The pieces were produced by the Allied Molding Corp. in Corona, New York. See *American Dollhouses and Furniture* for more photographs of Allied furniture ($15-20 each card). *From the collection of Judy Mosholder. Photograph by Gary Mosholder.*

The inside of the Fantasy house has two rooms on two floors, which were decorated with printed pictures, windows, curtains, rugs, and wall coverings. The original furniture included three beds and a dresser upstairs and a table and four chairs, sofa, coffee table, and lounge chair in the downstairs room. 10.5" high x 11.75" wide x 9" deep. *Photograph and house from the collection of Karen Steinmeier.*

Jaydon Molds

MIB plastic 3/4" to one foot scaled bedroom furniture made from the Jaydon molds. The original box gives no company name. Each of the boxes includes six pieces. It is not known when this furniture was made, but it could have been much later than when the original pieces were produced in the 1940s (boxed set $55+). *Furniture and photograph from the collection of Roy Specht.*

Boxed bathroom set made from the Jaydon molds. It includes a toilet, sink, bathtub, laundry hamper, and scale (boxed set $55-75). *Specht Collection.*

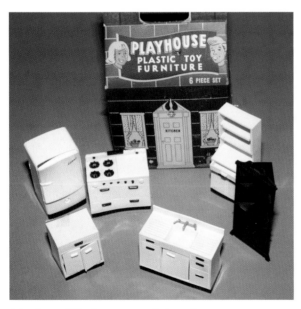

Boxed Jaydon mold kitchen pieces include a refrigerator, stove, two cabinets, sink, and corner hutch. Most of the items feature working doors or drawers (boxed set $55+). *Specht Collection.*

Child Life Toys, Inc.

"Dollyhome" manufactured by Child Life Toys, Inc., located in Seattle, Washington. The house was advertised in the 1957-58 Mihbaugh catalog from Sharon, Pennsylvania. It was made mostly of western cedar although some of the pieces used in the house were cardboard. The house was to be assembled by the consumer.

The "Dollyhome" came in two sizes: 26.5" wide x 16.5" deep and 42.25" wide x 24.25" deep. The larger house could be used with the furniture then being sold for 8" dolls. Pictured is the smaller version (MIB $45-50).

Mag-Powrs Games, Inc.

"Mary Mag-Powrs Magic Doll House" copyright 1963. The copy on the box reads, "The First Magnetic Action Dollhouse. It Comes to Life With the Touch of a Magic Wand." It was made by Mag-Powrs Games, Inc. of San Rafael, California. The house originally sold for $15.95 (MIB $100). *Photograph and house from the collection of Roy Specht.*

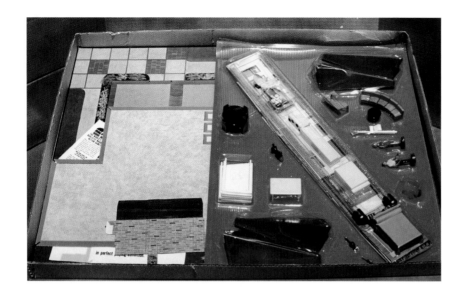

The Mag-Powrs dollhouse was to be assembled by the consumer. The parts included a pressed wood table, three ply acetate walls and shatter proof windows. Plastic furniture came with the house in a little smaller than 1/2" to one foot scale. The house included six rooms and a garage. *Specht Collection.*

Child Guidance

Magnetic Child Guidance house advertised in the Sears Christmas catalog in 1964. The five-room house came with over forty pieces of furniture and accessories. It sold for $3.97. It is similar to the Mary Mag-Powrs house.

Move family of 5 dolls from room to room as you watch through clear plastic roof

Magnetic House $3.97
Over 100 pieces

Point a Magic-Mover wand, and the magnetized doll-family glides into motion. Modern 5-room house with over 40 pieces of furniture and accessories can be arranged many ways. 15 walls, 2 removable roofs, trees, shrubs. Also 5 dolls and a snappy little car. 20x26-inch sturdy Masonite Presdwood base with 4 legs. Partly assembled.
79 N 1465C—Shipping weight 6 lbs.....$3.97

The Sears "Magnetic Doll House" was "a Child Guidance Toy." The "magic wand" was to be used to move the five piece dollhouse family from place to place. The house had a Masonite presdwood base with four legs ($75+). 20+ x 26". *Photograph and house from the collection of Ruth Petros.*

Multiple Products Corp.

$3.99

Unfold this Ranch House, and there are all the people

When a youngster's finished playing with the six delightful rooms full of plastic "Italian Provincial" furniture, this house closes up like a suitcase. Easy to tuck away. So complete, with 48 pieces of furniture and 7 doll figures. Nursery has a baby and everything a baby needs. Living room, dining room, bedroom, kitchen and bath fully equipped. House is chipboard. Open: 10x20x22 in.

79 N 1466L—Shipping wt. 3 lbs. **$3.99**

Ranch House featured in the Sears Christmas catalog in 1964. The house was made of chipboard and opened and closed like a suitcase. The house came with forty-eight pieces of plastic Multiple Products Corp. furniture in 3/4" to one foot scale and seven doll figures. Open measurements were 10" high x 20" wide x 22" deep. It sold for $3.99. It is thought that it was made by Miner Industries, Inc. of New York.

Fold Away Doll House No. 1610, circa early to mid 1960s. It is marked "Miner Industries Inc., N.Y." The closed vinyl case measures 10" high x 14" wide x 3" deep. *House from the collection of Arliss and Gene Morris. Photograph by Gene Morris.*

The "Fold Away" case opens to reveal five rooms furnished with 3/4" to one foot plastic Multiple Corporation furniture produced in Bronx, New York. The soft plastic furniture is marked "Multiple Products Inc. 1963" or "MPC" in a circle. Living room, nursery, kitchen, and bedroom pieces were included in the package ($35-45). When opened for play the house measures 3" high x 24" wide x 14" deep. *Morris Collection.*

Miner Industries also marketed this "Bend-A-Family's Model Home," circa mid to late 1960s. The set included a snap together plastic room with working door, tilt window, sliding picture window in front, eight pieces of Multiple Products soft plastic furniture, three "Bend-A-Family" dolls plus cardboard accessories. The Mother doll is missing from the set. The dolls were made in Hong Kong of flexible plastic and were 3/4" to one foot in scale. The set still has its original price tag of $1.00 ($20-25). 5.75" high x 11" wide x 8" deep.

Boxed set of 3/4" to one foot scaled Multiple Products Corp. plastic furniture. The box is dated 1966 and reads "Multiple Products of Bronx, New York 10462, A Division of Loral Corp." Kitchen, living room, and bedroom furniture was included in this inexpensive package that sold for 99 cents ($25). *Photograph and furniture from the collection of Roy Specht.*

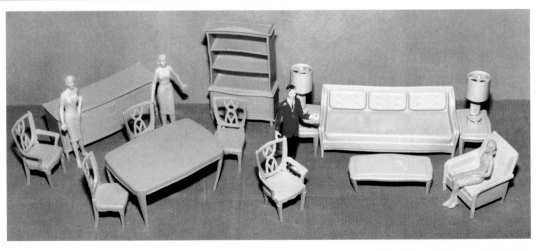

Multiple Products Corp furniture sets that were made in the 1960s to furnish a dining room and living room. The furniture came in a variety of colors (sets $10-15 each). *Specht Collection.*

PMC Limited

Three story Action Apartment House, circa 1971. It sold in the Sears Christmas catalog for $8.99. The building contained a battery operated elevator. It was made in Hong Kong by PMC Limited for Sears Roebuck (MIB $75). *Photograph and apartment from the collection of Roy Specht.*

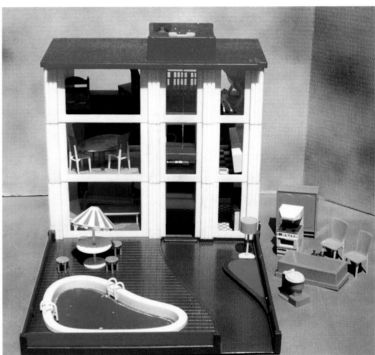

The apartment house came with thirty-five pieces of modern plastic 3/4" to one foot scale furniture and a patio and pool area. There were three plastic units that could be stacked to make a three story apartment house or be converted into three one story buildings. There were a total of six rooms in the structures. The red and white plastic stacked units and pool area measure 14" high x 14" wide x 20" deep. *Specht Collection.*

Arco Industries, Ltd.

Boxed set of Arco Merry Toys plastic furniture and family from 1980. The box is marked "1980 Arco Industries Ltd. New York, N.Y. Made in Hong Kong." The set includes plastic furniture in approximately 1/2" to one foot scale. Pieces are provided for a dining room, bedroom, and living room. A four piece dollhouse family is also included in the set ($35). *Photograph and furniture from the collection of Roy Specht.*

Arco Industries Ltd. hard plastic
kitchen and bathroom pieces in
1/2" to one foot scale. The doors
are functional. Each piece is
marked "Arco Ind. Ltd. Made in
Hong Kong." ($3-5 each piece).
Specht Collection.

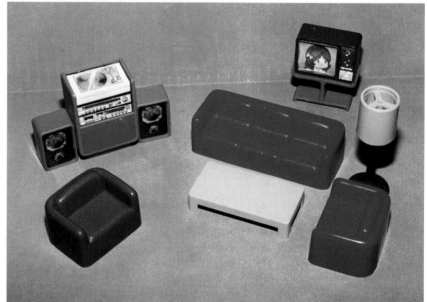

Arco Industries hard plastic living room pieces.
Even though the furniture is small, it is quite
realistic ($3-5 each piece). *Specht Collection.*

Hard plastic dining room furniture marketed
by Arco Industries in the 1/2" to one foot
scale ($3-5 each piece). *Specht Collection.*

Arco Industries bedroom furniture in the 1/2" to one foot scale, circa 1980 ($3-5 each piece). *Specht Collection.*

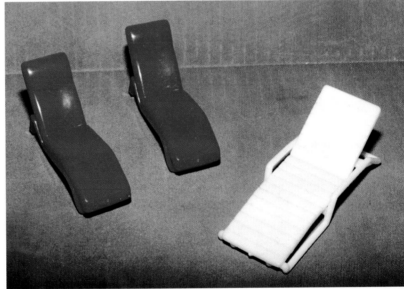

Hard plastic lounge furniture marketed by Arco Industries, circa 1980 ($3-5 each piece). *Specht Collection.*

IMCO

MIB IMCO 3/4" to one foot scaled plastic furniture made in Hong Kong in 1980. The information on the box states that the IMCO firm was located at 200 5th Ave. in New York City. The original price on the box was $8.99. *Specht Collection.*

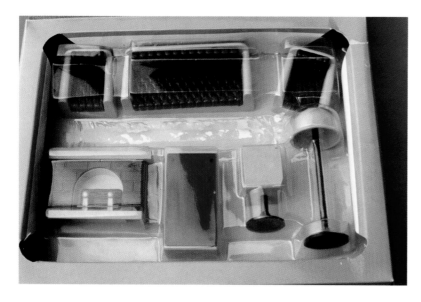

The plastic IMCO living room furniture included a sofa, two chairs, fireplace, coffee table, lamp, and television set (MIB $15-20). *Specht Collection.*

The IMCO bedroom furniture featured a bed, two night stands, a television, vanity and bench, and floor lamp (MIB $15-20). *Specht Collection.*

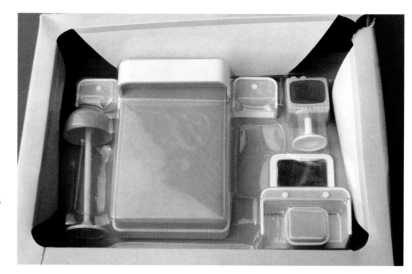

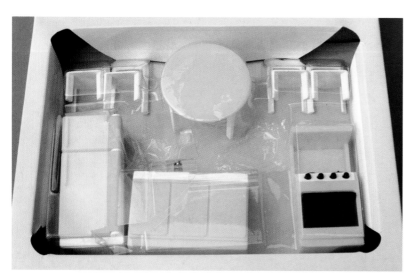

Plastic kitchen pieces marketed by IMCO in 1980 included a table, four chairs, refrigerator, sink, and stove (MIB $15-20). *Specht Collection.*

Wolverine Toy Co.

Wolverine Toy Co. wood dollhouse No. 840, circa 1980, produced in their later location in Booneville, Arkansas. The three story house was made of Masonite, plastic, and metal. It had a hinged front door, sliding door on the balcony, and a stairway. The five-room house could be purchased with or without the company's Bender family and furniture (unfurnished $75). 27.75" high x 23.75" wide x 15.25" deep. *Photograph and house from the collection of Roy Specht.*

Very special doll houses for very special little girls

A This year the Bender family has super vacation plans that include staying in their very own tri-level vacation home!

THE FAMILY: Father, mother and baby, all poseable.

THE DESIGN: Features a sundeck with planters and shrubbery, tinted "glass" windows and balcony with sliding "glass" doors. Interior is handy to both sides.

CONSTRUCTION: Made of masonite wood/high-impact plastic. Scale: 1 inch to 1 foot. 22¾x24½x25 inches high. Easy to assemble.

THE FURNITURE: Includes sets for den, dining room, bedroom, bathroom and kitchen, plus baby crib, 2 patio chairs and chaise.

AGES: 5 years and up.

48 G 62713 M—Ship. wt. 15 lbs. . . . . set 54.99

B Traditional two-story Town and Country manor with mother, father figures—for today's young homemaker.

THE DESIGN: True-to-life architectural details—bay window, multi-pane windows, shutters, window boxes.

CONSTRUCTION: Authentically detailed of sturdy steel and durable plastic. Hinged front door opens, shutters and window boxes are brightly lithographed. 22¾x12x17½ inches high.

THE FURNITURE: Plastic furniture for the living room, dining room, kitchen, master bedroom, children's bedroom and bathroom—over 30 pieces to enchant her.

AGES: 4 years to 10 years.

48 G 62712 M—Ship. wt. 7 lbs. 8 oz. . . . . set 19.99

Wolverine A-Frame dollhouse as pictured in the Montgomery Ward Christmas catalog for 1982. The house had three levels and could be accessed from both sides. It sold for $54.99 complete with the furniture and doll family. The house was 1" to one foot in scale.

Boxed sets of plastic Wolverine furniture produced for their 1" to one foot scaled houses of the 1980s. The furniture was actually a little larger than the 1" scale but it is very attractive. Sets were made for a dining room, kitchen, patio, den, bedroom, bathroom, nursery, first floor assortment, and second floor assortment. A boxed family set was also included, which featured mother, father, and baby dolls, all poseable (MIB each set $35-45). *Specht Collection.*

Wolverine A-Frame dollhouse No. 850, circa 1981-82. The house is made of Masonite, wood, and plastic. This 1" to one foot scaled house has three levels, with a living room, dining room, and kitchen on the first floor, sleeping area on the second floor, and a bathroom on the top level. A balcony and sundeck are also included with the house. For consumers who wanted a furnished house, a den set, dining room set, bedroom set, and kitchen set could also be purchased with the house. In addition, the Bender family, baby crib, and patio set were also included ($75 mostly unfurnished). 25" high x 22.75" wide x 24.5" deep. *Specht Collection.*

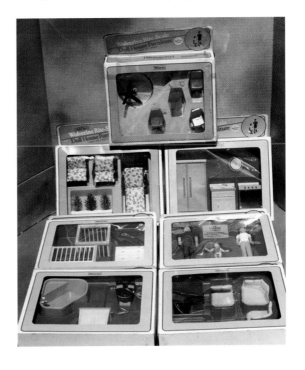

Chapter 4
English Dollhouses and Furniture

Since the publication of the earlier books, new examples of English houses and furniture have come to light. It is always nice to see additional examples of Lines, Triang, and Amersham houses as well as Pit-a-Pat, Kleeware, Dinky, Cresent, and Charbens furniture as shown in this chapter. The "Furnished Dollhouses" chapter also pictures several English houses complete with furniture.

Siber & Fleming Type

The front of the Siber and Fleming type house opens to allow access to its four rooms. Most of these houses were much smaller and featured only two rooms. The wallpaper appears to be original to the house and is in an oversized scale, which is typical for these types of houses. The fireplaces are also original. The house has been furnished as a kitchen, parlor, and two bedrooms. The furniture is mostly German along with some candy boxes. *Cathcart Collection.*

Siber and Fleming type house made in England, circa 1890-1900. These houses were made with box backs and flat fronts. The houses had flat roofs, often with a facade a little taller than the roof so the plain box type roof cannot be seen from the front. This house is a larger example than most of the Siber and Fleming type houses. It is decorated with two styles of "brick" on the front ($1,500-1,800). 26.5" high x 21" wide x 12" deep including base. *Photograph and house from the collection of Liz Cathcart.*

Evans & Cartwright

Evans & Cartwright English tinplate sofa, circa 1880s. It is in a large 1" to one foot scale. It has a pressed design typical of most of the firm's furniture (not enough examples to determine price). *Photograph and furniture from the collection of Ruth Petros.*

G. & J. Lines

English G.& J. Lines house No. 33, circa 1909-1910. The house features interesting cornices over the windows like those used on several of the early houses, as well as the "chunky" banisters often seen on the Lines houses. A widow's walk also adds to the architectural interest of the house. The house has been repainted and part of the roof and some of its railing have been replaced (with restoration $1,800-2,200). 33" high x 30" wide x 17.5" deep. *Photograph and house from the collection of Liz Cathcart.*

The front of the 1909-1910 Lines house opens in two sections to reveal four large rooms and two halls. The rooms have been furnished as a sitting room, bathroom, kitchen, and bedroom. The house still retains its original fireplaces but it has been redecorated. Most of the furniture is German, including an interesting tin washstand in the bedroom. *Cathcart Collection.*

English wood house made by the G.& J. Lines firm, circa 1909-1910. The house was featured in the company's catalog from that period and was labeled No. 9. The outside of the house is simulated yellow brick. The interesting architectural details above the windows are similar to those used on the Lines No. 33 house from the same period. The curved upstairs railings and simple entry design also add interest to the front of the house. The roof of this Lines house is flat (not enough examples to determine price). 37" high x 31" wide x 15" deep. *Photograph and house from the collection of Susan Singer.*

The inside of the house contains four rooms and two halls with high ceilings. A stairway was also included. The Welsh dresser in the kitchen and the fireplaces are original. *Singer Collection.*

Lines Bros.-Triangtois-Tri-ang

English Lines Brothers (Triangtois) house featured in their catalogs and pamphlets in the early 1920s. Two of those publications are pictured in Marion Osborne's article "A Guide to Tri-ang Dolls Houses Part III," featured in *Doll House and Miniature Scene* magazine. The house is shown in 1921 and late 1923 and early 1924 Lines Brothers publications. The roof has been papered to represent shingles and the front door is recessed to allow space for a small entry featuring benches on two sides ($1,800). 31" high x 31" wide x 20" deep. *Photograph and house from the collection of Ruth Petros.*

English Tri-ang two-room Cottage #DHA circa 1921. The "Tudor" house was made by Lines Brothers under the "Tri-ang Toys" trademark. Unlike many Tri-ang houses, this house does not include brick paper decorations (see "Furnished Houses" chapter). The entire house has been given a "rough texture" treatment and the roof is covered with a "tile" paper ($450-550). 17" high x 13" wide x 8" deep. *Photograph and house from the collection of Ruth Petros.*

The inside of the Triangtois house contains four large rooms and two smaller rooms or halls that feature the staircase. The four fireplaces are original to the house. Several rooms are papered with wallpaper that is identical to that used to decorate other Triangtois houses of the period. The house has been furnished with an assortment of furniture. Included are German Golden Oak, and metal pieces as well as German accessories. *Petros Collection.*

"Queens Doll House" offered by Triangtois from 1924 to 1930. The company catalog stated that "the house is an exact reproduction of the Dolls House furnished by her Majesty the Queen and given to a London Hospital for sale in support of their funds." The house has green card shutters and glass windows (the upstairs windows in this model are plastic and probably replaced). The house is made of wood with a rough cast finish on top and brick paper below the windows. The roof was given a thatched effect with the used of combed Gesso on plywood ($1,500-1,800). 22" high x 25" wide x 14" deep. *Photograph and house from the collection of Liz Cathcart.*

The back wall of the Queens house opens in two sections. The back of the roof lifts up in butterfly fashion to allow access to the upstairs. The inside of the house includes three rooms. Most of the wallpaper is original. The house has been furnished as a combination living, dining, and kitchen area plus a bedroom and bathroom upstairs. The furniture is a mix of handmade English and Hobbies pieces, along with German furniture and a Barrett & Sons stove with original pans. *Cathcart Collection.*

Unusual English Tri-ang one story house Model Q, circa 1928. The house has "card" shutters, applied roof paper in a "shingle" pattern, and an interesting stone design on the lower front ($1,200). 13" high x 25" wide x 13" deep. *Photograph and house from the collection of Linda Boltrek.*

The inside of the one-story Tri-ang house contains three rooms with what appears to be the original wallpaper. The fireplaces also appear to be original. *Boltrek Collection.*

English furniture marketed by Lines Brothers. The earlier pieces were made by the Erik Elgin firm of Enfield. The wood Jacobean furniture with a dark stain finish was in a 1" to one foot scale. The doors and drawers are functional. The Elgin factory closed in 1926 and Lines used their designs to produce their own furniture for several years. These pieces are not marked as to maker (bed $100, wardrobe $50+, chest $35-45). *Photograph and furniture from the collection of Leslie and Joanne Payne.*

The December 1935 *Meccano Magazine* carried this advertisement from the English Lines Brothers firm. It pictured many pieces of Tri-ang's two lines of wood dollhouse furniture then available. The furniture was advertised as being scale model reproductions of both Queen Anne and Jacobean styles. The pieces were 1" to one foot in scale and featured opening doors and drawers. Furniture was provided for living rooms, bedrooms, and dining rooms. An interesting "Queen Anne Period Scale Model Construction Set" was also advertised. The pieces were cut-out and were to be finished by the consumer. Stain, lacquer, upholstery, and instructions were provided to assemble the furniture.

Below:
Line Bros. Ltd. - Tri-ang advertisement in *The Meccano Magazine* for December 1935. Two dollhouses as well as other toys were featured. Included was the house collectors call the Stockbroker Tudor #72 (see *Furnished Dollhouses* for a photograph of the house) and a "Modern Dolls House No. 53." It came in four different sizes in this ad. *From the collection of Leslie and Joanne Payne.*

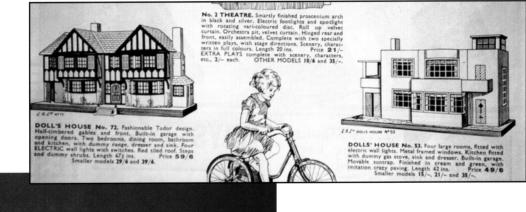

Tri-ang "Modern" house pictured in the *Meccano* advertisement in 1935. It has a flat roof, electric wall light, and metal framed windows. It is missing the sun trap from its roof. The house contains four rooms plus two halls ($700-800). 14" high x 26.5" wide x 10.75" deep. *House from the collection of Gail and Ray Carey. Photograph by Gail Carey.*

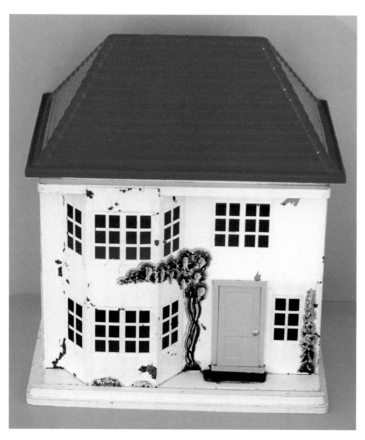

English Tri-ang wood house with a metal front and embossed plastic roof, circa 1964. The house has a sliding front that opens to reveal two rooms. The plastic roof is quite flimsy. Decals of flowers have been applied for decoration and are original. The house probably once had a chimney ($100-125). 16.5" high x 14" wide x 9.5" deep.

English Tri-ang "U" house, dating from 1964. It is made of fiberboard and wood frame construction and features plastic windows and door ($300-500). 21" high (with chimney) x 23.5" wide (including base) x 15" deep. *Photograph and house from the collection of Liz Cathcart.*

The "U" Tri-ang house is open backed and contains four modern rooms. The house is mostly furnished with Tri-ang Spot-on plastic and metal furniture from the period. The dolls (except for the man) were also marketed by Tri-ang. The rooms have been furnished as a kitchen, living room, bathroom, and combination bedroom and nursery (See "Furnished Houses" chapter for more photographs of "Spot-on" furniture). *Cathcart Collection.*

Candy Container

English wood candy container, circa early 1900s, used by some collectors as furniture for dollhouses. The cabinet is 5" tall and has an opening door and drawer, both with lithographed designs ($50-75). *Photograph and cabinet from the collection of Ruth Petros.*

The English candy container was filled with Fry's Chocolate and still carries its original sticker. Most of the candy containers were made of cardboard (see German chapter). *Petros Collection.*

Westacre Village

Westacre Village bookcase, circa 1920s. The furniture was made in England in the village of Westacre, Norfolk. According to Margaret Towner in her *Dollhouse Furniture* book, a cottage industry was set up by Mrs. Burkbeck to make the antique styled miniature furniture. Finish on the furniture included black, red, green, and brown. Many of the pieces were decorated in gilt. The lamps featured hand painted parchment shades. The furniture was made of a cardboard type material. Over forty different items were produced according to the *International Dolls House News*. *Photograph and furniture from the collection of Ruth Petros.*

Dinky Toys

Advertisement for Dinky Toys "Doll's House Furniture" which appeared in *The Meccano Magazine*, circa mid 1930s. The cast metal furniture was produced by Meccano Ltd., located in Liverpool, England, during the 1930s. The furniture was approximately 1/2" to one foot in scale. There were four rooms of the small furniture, which included pieces for a dining room, bedroom, kitchen, and bathroom. There was no living room furniture, evidently because the cardboard Dolly Varden house the firm sold to use with the furniture contained only four rooms. The house measured 18.75" high x 18.75" wide x 10.25" deep. The container for the house could be used as a base and lawn, complete with a tennis court. The houses are very hard to find and, therefore, are expensive for a collector to buy. *From the collection of Leslie and Joanne Payne.*

The set of Dinky dining room furniture included a table, sideboard with opening doors, two chairs with arms, and four straight chairs. This set is missing one straight chair. The furniture came in only walnut finish, according to the *Meccano Magazine* ad ($100-125 set). *Photograph and furniture from the collection of Patty Cooper.*

The Dinky Toys kitchen featured a refrigerator, kitchen cabinet, electric cooker, table and chair. The pieces could be purchased in either light blue and white or light green and cream. The doors function (set $125+). *Cooper Collection.*

The English Dinky Toys bedroom furniture included a bed, wardrobe, dressing table, dressing chest, stool, and chair. The chair is not pictured. The furniture contained opening doors and drawers. The bedroom furniture also came in a walnut finish (set $100-125). *Cooper Collection.*

The Dinky bathroom furniture could be purchased in color combinations of pink and white or light green and white. The pieces included a bathtub, pedestal hand basin, toilet, linen basket (opens), stool, and bathmat, which is not pictured (set $100-125). *Cooper Collection.*

Pit-a-Pat

Pit-a-Pat English furniture made by the E. Lehman & Co. of London, circa 1930s. The furniture ranged in size from 3/4" to 1" to one foot in scale. Most of the furniture was marked either with a stamp or a label (See 1930s section of "Furnished Houses" chapter for more examples). Pictured are a deck chair ($20-25), kitchen cabinet ($35-45), table and chairs (set $45+), and screen ($25-35). *Private Collection.*

Charbens

Charbens & Co. cast metal fireplace, circa 1930s. The Charbens firm was located in London and marketed small scale (approximately 1/2" to one foot) cast metal furniture during the 1930s. The fireplace is marked "CHARBENS/ MADE IN ENGLAND" ($35+). *Photograph and furniture from the collection of Evangeline Steinmeier.*

Bex Molding

Dining room sideboard and living room chairs in 3/4" to one foot scale "Made in England," circa late 1930s. The sideboard is made of Bakelite and was part of the "Toy Town Furniture" which used the trade name "Bex Molding" according to Margaret Towner in her book *Dollhouse Furniture*. The pieces were produced by the British Xylonite Co. Ltd. beginning in 1937. According to a catalog page from 1939, the furniture came in walnut, blue, red, or green. All of the furniture was Art Deco in style. The two chairs are marked "Seaforth/Made in England" and are also made of a similar plastic. *Photograph and furniture from the collection of Roy Specht.*

Amersham

English Amersham house, circa late 1940s. The house includes a garage. The roof features overlapping strips of wood to represent shingles and lattice style opening windows with fixed transoms at the top. Like most of the Amersham houses, this one has a Tudor look ($550+). 26" wide x 12" deep, including base. *Photograph and house from the collection of Evangeline Steinmeier.*

The inside of the Amersham house contains four rooms with a stairway. It is possible that this house has been redecorated since there is no wallpaper in two of the rooms. The house was purchased in England complete with plastic furniture that included Kleeware pieces (see "Furnished Houses" chapter for another example of an Amersham house). *Steinmeier Collection.*

Unidentified plastic living room furniture in 3/4" to one foot scale that was in the Amersham house when it was purchased in England (set $35). *Steinmeier Collection*.

Plastic dining room table and chairs decorated with decals, circa late 1940s. This furniture was also in the Amersham house when it was purchased and was probably made in England by the same firm who produced the living room and bedroom furniture that came with the house (set $35). *Steinmeier Collection*.

The 3/4" to one foot plastic bedroom furniture that accompanied the Amersham house to the United States was also trimmed with decals. Although the living room, bedroom, and table and chairs were not marked, other furniture in the house was marked Kleeware ($35-40). *Steinmeier Collection*.

Kleeware

English hard plastic Kleeware bathroom furniture made by O. & M. Kleemann Ltd., circa 1948. The furniture is 3/4" to one foot in scale and was made using the same molds as those used to produce the Renwal furniture in the United States. The pieces are marked "Kleeware Made in England." This furniture came in the English Amersham house pictured earlier (set $45-50). *Photograph and furniture from the collection of Evangeline Steinmeier.*

Other plastic Kleeware pieces were also included as part of the Amersham house's furnishings when it was purchased in England. The dining room hutch (marked Kleeware) was produced using the same mold as that used by the United States Renwal firm. The piano and bench were apparently made from a newer Kleeware design. The radio is also marked "Kleeware Made in England" (piano and bench $20+, hutch $15, radio $10). *Steinmeier Collection.*

Plastic kitchen furniture, marked Kleeware, identical to American Renwal products. All of this furniture is 3/4" to one foot in scale. The Kleeware firm's dollhouse furniture was discontinued circa 1959 (Set $35-40). *Steinmeier Collection.*

Crescent Toy Co.

English MIB cast metal Cooker Stove made by Crescent Toy Co. Ltd., circa 1950s. The box is labeled "Scale Model/Gas Cooker/ Crescent Toys/Made in England." The stove is approximately 1" to one foot in scale and is marked "No. 1211." The oven door opens and there are removable racks ($50-75+). *Photograph and stove from the collection of Patty Cooper.*

A. Barton & Co.

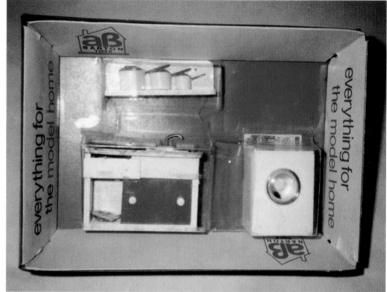

MIB English A. Barton & Co. kitchen set, circa 1970s. It includes a sink unit, shelf complete with pots and pans, and an automatic washing machine. Other sets made by the firm at the time included kitchen, dining room, nursery, bathroom, bedroom, and living room pieces. A stove was usually paired with the washing machine. See *Antique and Collectible Dollhouses* for more examples. The furniture was a small 3/4" to one foot in scale (MIB set $40-50). *Photograph and furniture from the collection of Evangeline Steinmeier.*

Dol-Toi

The English Dol-Toi firm marketed a line of wood dollhouse furniture with metal legs, circa 1964-65. Pictured are pieces for the bedroom and dining room. The bed and wardrobe appear to be in a larger scale than the rest of the furniture. Most of the items are in a 3/4" to one foot scale. The doors and drawers are functional. The mirror has been replaced. See Furnished Houses section for more examples of Dol-Toi products (each set $35-45).

Chapter 5

German Dollhouses and Furniture

This chapter includes information and examples of products from German firms not featured in previous books. Elastolin, Reichel, and several more recent East and West German companies are included. In addition, more houses are pictured from the Gottschalk and Wagner companies as well as boxed sets of German furniture and additional examples of Biedermeier and other early German furniture. The "Furnished Dollhouses" chapter features many more Gottschalk houses as well as other examples of German houses and furniture.

Christian Hacker

Unusual Christian Hacker house with an attached garage. The presence of the garage indicates that this house was made circa 1914. In addition to the garage, the house has a glassed conservatory, an added veranda, three porches, and is topped with a widow's walk. The front of the house can be removed and is displayed on the wall behind the front section. It fits behind the two porches. The house contains four large rooms and two halls in addition to the conservatory. It is furnished with exceptionally fine pieces of Biedermeier furniture. The light fixtures in the house are especially appealing. Several of the ornate fixtures include Bristol shades. German Biedermeier furniture has been used in both bedrooms and the parlor. The dollhouse dolls in the house are also exceptional. A chauffeur stands by the car in the garage and a Simon & Halbig "Little Women" doll can be seen in the upstairs. The "yard" includes an outdoor pump (not enough examples to determine price). 35" high plus 11.5" for widow's walk x 56" wide x 30.5" deep. *From the collection of Angels Attic. Photograph by Jeff Carey.*

Moritz Gottschalk

Early German Gottschalk lithographed paper over wood house, circa early 1900s. The two-story house features a porch and two matching chimneys ($1,800-2,000). 20" high x 16" wide x 9" deep. *Photograph and house from the collection of Ruth Petros.*

The inside of the lithographed Gottschalk house contains three rooms complete with original wallpaper and paper fireplaces. The fireplaces add an unusual touch not seen in many houses. The floor coverings are also original. The house has been furnished with an assortment of small metal furniture including pieces from the United States and Germany. *Petros Collection.*

Advertisement from Nerlich & Co. for the holiday season of 1924. Pictured are two houses made by the Gottschalk firm. According to the copy, the "brick" house came in three sizes: 16", 19" and 20.5" high. Although the house appears to be what collectors call a "Blue Roof" house, the copy stated the houses had red roofs. Each example came complete with furniture. The Bungalow also was made in a variety of sizes from 14" to 21" high. These houses also were sold with furniture. The lithographed house was pictured in the Gottschalk catalog in 1908 (evidently with a blue roof) and the Bungalow appeared in company advertising in 1921.

Gottschalk lithographed over wood dollhouse like the one pictured in the 1924 advertisement from Nerlich & Co. This 1908 example (pictured in the Cieslik *Moritz Gottschalk 1892-1931* book) came with the more usual blue roof instead of red. The lithographed paper supplies most of the architectural details ($1,500+). *Photograph and house from the collection of Linda Boltrek.*

Gottschalk "Red Roof" two-room house from 1913. The shutters are missing from the front of the house and the chimneys may have been replaced. The front opens to reveal one room. A side opening allows access to the small second floor room ($650-700 with missing shutters). 17" high x 14" wide x 8" deep. *Photograph and house from the collection of Linda Boltrek.*

Above and right:
Gottschalk hexagonal "Red Roof" house, circa 1914-1915. It originally came with Gottschalk furniture. The house contains four rooms and is open on the sides that contain rooms. This house has been furnished mostly with German furniture and accessories. *From the collection of Angels Attic. Photographs by Jeff Carey.*

Small Gottschalk "Red Roof" house, circa 1924. The chimney is missing. The house includes a small roof overhang above the door and a porch with a very plain enclosure ($500-600). 19" high x 9" wide x 8" deep. *Photograph and house from the collection of Ruth Petros.*

The small 1924 front opening "Red Roof" contains only one room. It has been furnished with a German table and chairs in approximately 1/2" to one foot in scale. *Petros Collection.*

Gottschalk "Red Roof," circa 1924. It includes an interesting porch, die-cut pressed cardboard windows, and a dormer on the roof. The house is missing its chimney and the flower box under the front window. The inside of the house includes one room downstairs and one room upstairs in the attic ($450-500). 14" high x 12" wide x 10.5" deep. *Photograph and house from the collection of Gail and Ray Carey.*

Gottschalk "Red Roof" house featuring a garage, circa 1925. Besides the garage, the house also includes side porches on both the first and second floors. The architectural details give the house somewhat of a Tudor look ($1,700+). 23" high to top of chimney, 24" wide x 12" deep not including steps. *Carey Collection.*

The front of the 1925 Red Roof opens to allow access to its four rooms. Two of the rooms are large while the other smaller rooms might be considered halls. The stairway is located in the downstairs "hall." There is an attic on the third floor. The wall and floor coverings appear to be original. *Carey Collection.*

Gottschalk furniture as pictured in their 1925 catalog according to reprints shown in the *Moritz Gottschalk 1892-1931* book. The 1" to one foot scale furniture is made of wood with added upholstery (set $500+). *Photograph and furniture from the collection of Gail and Ray Carey.*

Gazebo attributed to the German Moritz Gottschalk firm, circa 1915. The structure includes a four-sided roof, flowers, vines, trellis across the top, railings, and steps. It has been furnished with pieces of wood outdoor furniture ($1,300). 12" high x 18" wide x 9" deep. *Photograph and gazebo from the collection of Ruth Petros.*

Rooms

German double room box that includes furniture for both a parlor and a dining room. The blue dining room includes a rare set of German tinplate furniture made by the German Rock and Graner firm in the 1800s. The furniture is 1" to one foot in scale. The accessories in the room are also special. Ormolu lamps, pictures, and matching mirrors are just some of the many items used to make a very special setting for the three china head German dolls who inhabit the space. The wallpaper and floor covering is original (not enough examples to determine price). *From the collection of Angels Attic. Photograph by Jeff Carey.*

The smaller room in the room box has been furnished as a parlor with German tin plate furniture. A sofa, five matching chairs, piano (not pictured), desk, and corner shelf make up most of the furnishings in the room. The tall window curtains feature old metal tie-backs. *Angel's Attic Collection. Photograph by Jeff Carey.*

Box for German cardboard room, circa 1900. It is marked "Gesetzlich Geschutzt." *Photograph and box from the collection of Ruth Petros.*

The cardboard German room uses the lid of the box for its floor. The bottom of the box becomes the back wall with the side walls folding into place. It is not known if the furniture is original ($300). 7" high x 21" wide x 16" deep. *Petros Collection.*

German room box that may have been made by the Gottschalk firm, circa 1910. The wallpaper and floor coverings are original. Unlike most room boxes, this one has a platform trimmed with columns and railings to enclose a sitting area or a bed. Most of the furniture in the room is a scroll-cut German design upholstered in silk upholstery ($800 unfurnished). 10" high x 25" wide x 11" deep. *Petros Collection.*

German room boxes were still being sold in 1924. In this Nerlich & Co. holiday catalog, three different furnished rooms were offered: sitting room, bedroom, and kitchen. The rooms varied in size from 8-9.5" high x 18-21.5" wide x 8"-9" deep. The rooms had wood frames comprising three walls and flooring plus glass windows and curtains. The sides of the rooms were hinged so they could fold flat. Each room came with six or seven pieces of wood furniture.

Furnished Rooms

75/38

75/38. Furnished Sitting Room. Wood frame comprising three walls and flooring showing interior of room decorated with wall paper and imitation linoleum, outside painted, two glass windows with real muslin curtains, sides are hinged together and fold flat; contains seven-piece wood sitting room furniture, four pieces being upholstered; size set up: length 18 inches, width 8 inches, height 8 inches; each in box. .... Each **$2.50**

75/39. Furnished Bedroom, as 75/38 but larger and fitted with seven pieces bedroom furniture, including two single beds; length 21½ inches, width 9 inches, height 9½ inches; each in box. .... Each **$3.50**

75/41. Furnished Kitchen, wood frame comprising three walls and flooring, painted outside, decorated inside with wallpaper and paper floor covering, contains six pieces wood kitchen furniture painted in blue and white; length 19½ inches, width 9 inches, height 9½ inches; each in box. .... Each **$3.00**

German kitchen room, circa 1920s. The bottom of the back wall is decorated with unusual paper featuring dachshund dogs. Most of the white furniture is original to the room but many of the accessories have been added over the years ($1,000-1,200). *Photograph and kitchen from the collection of Leslie and Joanne Payne.*

Early German Furniture

German Rock & Graner pressed tinplate sofa, circa 1860. This Victorian styled sofa with tufted upholstery is in a large 1" to one inch scale ($1,600+). *Photograph and sofa from the collection of Dollhouse and Miniature Museum of Cape May.*

Right:
Early German Biedermeier-Waltershausen 1" to one foot furniture from the nineteenth century. The cabinet has been decorated with ornate gilt transfers and includes working parts. The unusual table features silver landscapes on its top and more intricate gold designs around the edges. The ornate legs are made of metal (cabinet $250+, table $400+). *Photograph and furniture from the collection of Ruth Petros.*

Pressed tinplate outdoor furniture attributed to the German firm of Rock & Graner. The furniture is in a large 1" to one foot scale. The firm ceased operations circa 1904 (not enough examples to determine price). *Photograph and furniture from the collection of Ruth Petros.*

Early ten piece lacquered tinplate parlor set, perhaps made by the German Marklin firm. Although the basic design is based on the bentwood style, many more curly decorations have been added (not enough examples to determine price). *Photograph and furniture from the collection of Leslie and Joanne Payne.*

More unusual Biedermeier furniture in a 1" to one foot scale, circa 1900. The writing desk has opening doors, and both the desk and the mirrored piece have "marble" tops. All three pieces have been finished with a variety of gilt transfers (desk $250, other pieces $150-200 each). *Photograph and furniture from the collection of Evangeline Steinmeier. The furniture originally belonged to her grandmother.*

Right:
German Biedermeier parlor set in a 1" to one foot scale. The table has a marble top. Although the sofa is smaller in scale than the chairs, it was part of the original set. The gilt transfers and gold trim around the upholstery add to the appeal of the furniture (set $600+). *Steinmeier collection (from her grandmother).*

German Biedermeier bedroom furniture in a small 1" to one foot scale. Again the gilt transfers add interest to relatively plain wood furniture designs. Both the mirrored chest and wardrobe include moving parts. The chest features a marble top ($150-200 each). *Steinmeier Collection.*

German wood bedroom furniture usually called "Golden Oak" by collectors, circa 1900-1910. The three bigger pieces are in a large 1" to one foot scale while the smaller cabinet is a large 3/4" to one foot scale. The furniture was probably made by the German Gebruder Schneegas firm. The wash stand and cabinet have "marble" tops with functional doors and drawers. The wardrobe and bed were decorated with matching circles on their cornices ($150-250 each). *Steinmeier Collection.*

Candy Boxes

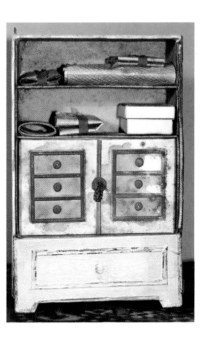

Cardboard candy box, circa 1910, that could be used as dollhouse furniture. The original items on the shelves are still tied in place with ribbon. This cabinet box (with openings to hold the candy) is attributed to Germany although it is known that others were marketed in England (see English chapter) and France. 5" high x 3.25" wide ($185). *Photograph and cabinet from the collection of Ruth Petros.*

Cardboard candy boxes, circa 1915-1920. The piano top lifts off to reveal space to house candy (3" high x 3.5" wide). The bottom of the desk is removable, which allowed access to the candy once found inside (3.25" high x 4" wide). The sticker on the bottom of the desk reads "The Broadway Toy Shop/ 820 Broadway N.Y." ($25-45 each). *Petros Collection.*

The most common types of "dollhouse furniture" candy boxes are those with the floral decorations. Several different patterns of the design were produced. These probably date from the 1920s and perhaps into the early 1930s. None of the pieces are marked so their origin is unknown. The table top can be opened to access the space where candy once was housed. The bottoms of the other items can be removed to reveal the candy container. The chairs are 3.25" high ($20-25 each). *Petros Collection.*

Boxed gilt metal "My Doll's Furniture Set," marked on the box "Made in Germany." The pieces are in a small 1/2" to one foot scale but are quite attractive. The set is still tied into its original box (MIB $85+). *Photograph and furniture from the collection of Ruth Petros.*

Elastolin

German Elastolin cabin, circa 1920s, on its own base. This firm marketed many different structures, which always included accessories. The pieces were made of a composition or papier mâché material. Animals, people, and trees were included in the sets. This open backed house has only one room ($350-400). The base measures 10" high x 21.5" wide x 13" deep. *Photograph and house from the collection of Ruth Petros.*

Unidentified German Houses

The 1929 Butler Brothers catalog advertised two different German dollhouses. They were made of fiber with wood frames and each featured a side opening to access the one room inside. *From the collection of Marge Meisinger. Photograph by Suzanne Silverthorn.*

Two German fiber and wood houses, very similar to those advertised in the Butler Brothers catalog. The houses are stamped "Made in Germany" on the bottoms. Gold house: 9.5" high x 9.75" wide x 9.75" deep. Orange house: 7.5" high x 9" wide x 9" deep ($250-300 each). *Photograph and houses from the collection of Nancy Roeder.*

Moritz Reichel

Reichel dollhouse made by the German firm of C. Moritz Reichel, circa 1930s. It is stamped "Made in Germany" on the bottom with no number. Although the house is very similar to those made by the German Gottschalk firm, the shutters and porch railings are very different ($750-1,000). 14.5" high x 14" wide x 8" deep. *Photograph and house from the collection of Patty Cooper.*

The front of the house opens to reveal one room on the main floor. The attic room is accessible through the opening door in the gable. The house includes its original wallpaper and floor covering. *Cooper Collection.*

Moko

German "Moko" dollhouse, circa 1930s. The original label on the front reads "The Moko Series. Foreign Manufacture." The house was recently purchased in England. It was originally imported into England by "Moko." Moses Kohnstam (originally from Germany) used the "Moko" trademark in his business as a toy distributor in England in the 1930s. The house appears to be one of a series of German houses collectors refer to as Wagner. The houses are believed to have a connection to the German D.H. Wagner & Sohn firm. This house has four rooms, original papers, stairway, and a garage ($750-1,000). 18" high x 21" wide x 12" deep. *Photograph and house from the collection of Patty Cooper.*

D.H. Wagner & Sohn

German house, circa 1930s, called Wagner by collectors. It has the typical "Wagner" stenciling on the roof and the Tudor markings also found on some of these houses. The front door is also unique to the "Wagner." The card windows have been repaired ($500-600). 15" high x 13" wide x 8" deep. *Photograph and house from the collection of Liz Cathcart.*

The front of the house opens to reveal two rooms. The floor coverings are original but the wallpapers are probably replacements. *Cathcart Collection.*

Very small scale German dollhouse (perhaps Wagner) with gable on left and dormer on right, circa 1930s. It is stamped "foreign" on the bottom and was purchased in England. The windows and door are lithographed decals. The Tudor "half-timbering" in the front gable is stenciled. There are four very small rooms inside, which may have been made from dividing one original large room ($500). 11" high x 12" wide x 6.5" deep. *Photograph and house from the collection of Patty Cooper.*

Small "Wagnerish" looking house purchased in England. It is unmarked. This house has stenciling on the gable on the right side of the house and also on the roof. A flowing vine is painted on the front. There is an arched opening to a porch on the left. The window mullions are pressed cardboard over lace curtains. The windows aren't actually cut out, just painted ($400+). 13.5" high x 9.25" wide x 5" deep. *Cooper Collection.*

This circa 1930s German house also has the look of a Wagner but is unmarked. The printing on the front reads "Villa Edelweis." The outside is decorated with shutters and flower boxes. The front of the house opens to reveal two rooms ($800). 18" high x 14.5" wide x 10" deep. *Photograph and house from the collection of Ruth Petros.*

The Wagner type house opens from the front to reveal three rooms including the porch. It was purchased furnished with small French metal furniture. *Cooper Collection.*

German Furniture 1920s-1940s

German "Red Stain" dining room wood furniture in 1" to one foot scale, circa 1920s. The pieces are incised "Germany." The cabinet features two functional doors and the table is a drop-leaf design. Three of the upholstered chairs have arms while two do not (set $175).

This German Red Stain 1" to one foot scale bedroom set was apparently made by the same firm. These pieces are also incised "Germany." The doors are functional on the furniture (set $175+). *Photograph and furniture from the collection of Marilyn Pittman.*

The same unknown German firm also produced similar Red Stain furniture in 3/4" to one foot scale. The piano in this picture is also incised with "Germany" on its bottom. The other items are not marked but appear to be Red Stain German pieces, circa 1920s (set $100-125).

Although this six piece, circa late 1920s-early 1930s, 3/4" to one foot scale dining room set is not marked, it also came from Germany. The sideboard includes one functional drawer (set $100).

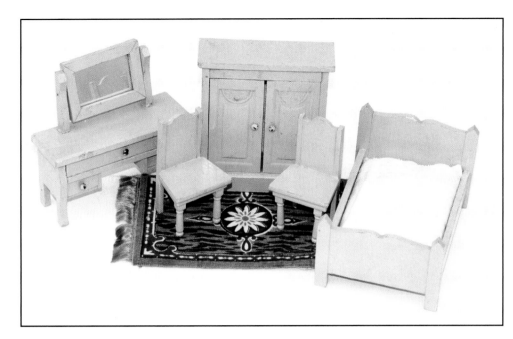

German 3/4" to one foot scale bedroom furniture that includes chairs made exactly like the Red Stain dining room chairs of the same size. Several of the pieces in this set are stamped "Germany." This set is enameled instead of stained. The doors and drawers are functional (set $100-125).

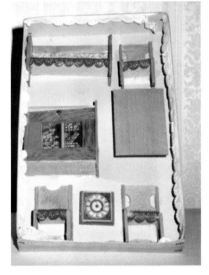

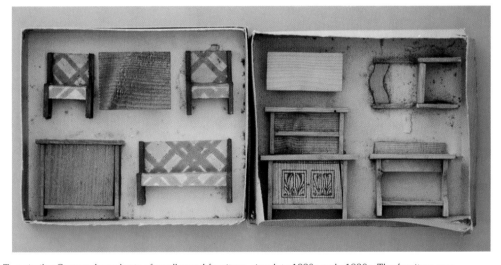

Boxed set of small 3/4" to one foot wood and paper German furniture. The set appears to date from the late 1920s to the early 1930s. It includes a settee, three chairs, table, bookcase, and clock. The seats on the furniture are paper over wood (MIB $50-65). *Photograph and furniture from the collection of Ruth Petros.*

Two similar German boxed sets of small wood furniture, circa late 1920s-early 1930s. The furniture was cheaply made of thin wood and cardboard. It ranges in size from 1/2" to 3/4" to one foot in scale. All of the furniture was evidently produced by the same company. Both boxes are stamped "Made in Germany." The decorated parts of the sofa and two chairs are made of cardboard (MIB $35 each).

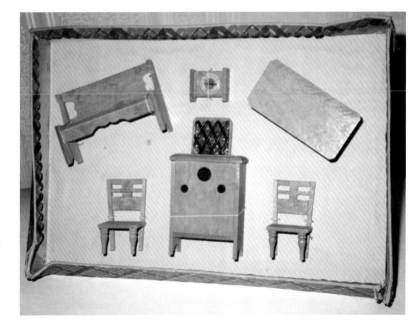

Boxed German living room furniture in 3/4" to one foot scale, circa 1930s. The wood set includes a sofa, table, two chairs, clock, and radio (MIB $65). *Photograph and furniture from the collection of Ruth Petros.*

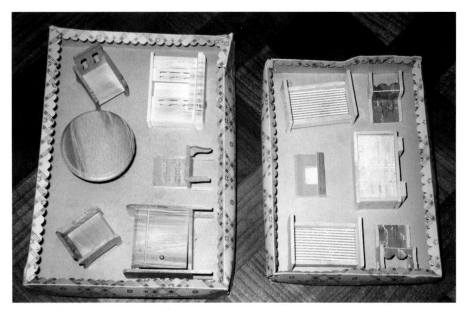

Two inexpensive boxed sets of furniture thought to be from Germany, circa 1930s-1940s. The pieces include an assortment of scales but most of the furniture is a small 3/4" to one foot in scale. The boxes include pieces for a bedroom and a dining room (MIB $50 each). *Petros Collection.*

West and East German Companies

West German bedroom, circa 1960s. It is furnished with plastic furniture in 3/4" to one foot scale. The doors and drawers are functional. It is marked "Made in W. Germany." Several different rooms were made in the series ($45 furnished room). *Photograph and room from the collection of Ruth Petros.*

West German bathroom furnished with 3/4" to one foot scaled plastic furniture. Each of the rooms came complete with accessories. A living room and dining room were also produced ($45 furnished room). *Petros Collection.*

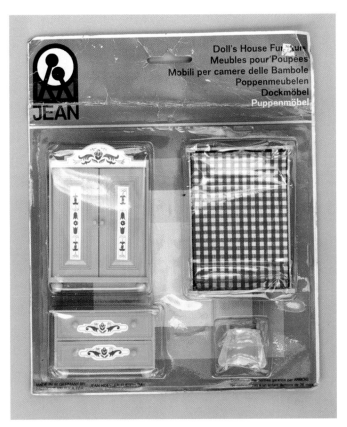

"Jean" large 1 1/4" to one foot scale plastic and metal table and chairs still on the original card. The set is similar in size to the Ideal Young Decorator pieces. The card is marked "Jean Plastic/Made in Western Germany." ($35+).

"Jean" plastic bedroom furniture in original package. It is marked "Made in West Germany by FABRIQUE EN R.F.A. PAR/JEAN EAN HOEFLER FUERTH/BAY." The set includes a bed, rocker, wardrobe, and chest. The doors and drawers are functional. The furniture is in a 3/4" to large 3/4" to one foot scale (Mint $25).

"Jean" plastic dining room furniture in 3/4" to one foot scale. The pieces are marked with the JEAN trademark as well as "W. Germany." The doors and drawers are functional (set $15-20).

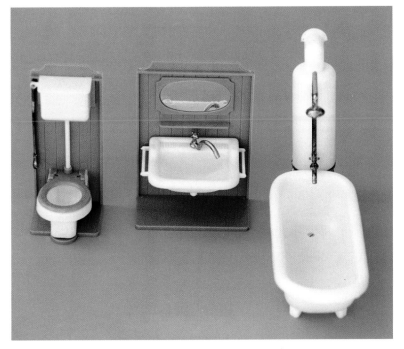

"Jean" old-fashioned plastic set of bathroom furniture in a large 3/4" to one foot scale. The JEAN trademark AND "W. Germany" appear in a circle on the back of the sink (set $20).

Small 3/4" to one foot plastic baby items marked "Made in W. Germany." The set includes a stroller, crib, high chair, and baby (set $20).

Wood and plastic boxed furniture in a 3/4" to one foot scale, circa 1960s. The box is marked "Kitty/PUPPENMÖBEL/Made in Western Germany" (boxed set $35+). *Photograph and furniture from the collection of George Mundorf.*

"Kitty/PUPPENMÖBEL" West German 3/4" to one foot scale boxed wood living room furniture with fuzzy covering on chairs and couch, circa 1960s. The television and table are made of wood and plastic. This box is also marked "Made in Western Germany" (boxed set $35+). *Furniture from the collection of Arliss and Gene Morris. Photograph by Gene Morris.*

West German boxed living room furniture circa 1960s. The furniture included both wood and upholstered pieces in a 3/4" to one foot scale (boxed set $35+). *Photograph and furniture from the collection of Ruth Petros.*

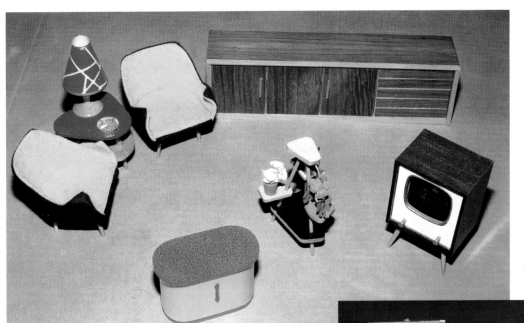

West German living room furniture in a large 1" to one foot scale, circa 1967-68. The television lights with the use of batteries. The lamp also works. The size of the furniture is similar to that of Ideal's Young Decorator pieces (set $45-50). *Photograph and furniture from the collection of Roy Specht.*

The large scaled West German kitchen furniture is especially nice. The set includes a refrigerator, sink, stove, and stool (set $50). *Specht Collection.*

The large scaled wood West German dining room furniture includes a table, five chairs, and a sideboard. The doors function on this furniture (set $45-50). *Specht Collection.*

This line of large scaled West German furniture also included furniture for the patio. A lounge, chair, and umbrella table were featured in the set. Toy stores in the United States carried this line of furniture circa 1967-68 (set $45-50). *Specht Collection.*

Wood playground set made in West Germany. It includes a climbing ladder, swing, sand pile, and slide. The swing is 6" high, slide 5" tall, and sandbox 3.75" square (set $40-50). *Photograph and playground set from the collection of Becky Norris.*

Cover of circa 1960s boxed living room furniture made in East Germany. The box name reads "HUBSCH" #339/7. Marked "Made in East Germany." *Norris Collection.*

The living room furniture contained in the "HUBSCH" box does not look like that pictured on the box lid. This furniture is made of wood and is in a 1" to one foot scale. The doors on the furniture are functional and the television picture features two teddy bears. The sofa and chairs are upholstered with cotton material. (set $50+). *Norris collection.*

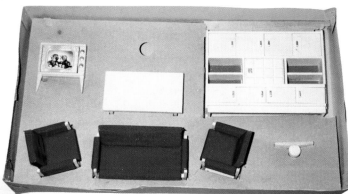

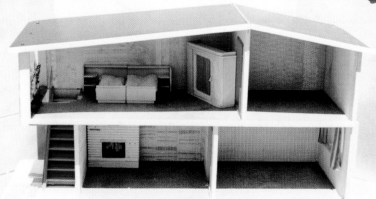

German house that is exactly like the one pictured on the cover of the "HUBSCH" furniture box. It is marked "Vero/Made in Germany." It was evidently made in East Germany since that is where the boxed furniture was produced. The house has an outside stairway and four large rooms. It looks very similar to other houses from the period that were made in West Germany, as well as the Lundby houses from Sweden ($75 unfurnished). 15" high x 29.5" wide x 10" deep. *Photograph and house from the collection of Roy Specht.*

Chapter 6
Japanese Dollhouse and Furniture

Japan was active in the production and exportation of dollhouse furniture for much of the twentieth century. The products were usually priced cheaply and were sold through wholesale and mail order catalogs as well as in local "dime stores." Many collectors shy away from these products but much of the furniture is quite attractive, especially when it is still in its original box or packaging. Some of the Japanese furniture appears to be copied from other sources. This practice sometimes offers collectors a surprise when they turn over a piece of "Gottschalk" furniture and see a "Japan" mark. The Japanese were fine craftsmen and many United States firms eventually turned over production of their dollhouse furniture to them. Ideal's Petite Princess plastic furniture was produced in Japan, as were many of the Shackman miniatures.

Japan also produced lines of furniture and houses (temples) reflecting their own culture. A temple of this type is pictured in this chapter.

Large 1" to one foot outdoor Japanese furniture made of bamboo with imitation cane seats. Similar to a set advertised in the Montgomery Ward catalog in 1903. The Montgomery Ward set may have been in a smaller scale as it was priced at only 25 cents for the six piece set. Marked "Made in Japan." This type furniture was made in several different scales (set $50-75). *Photograph and furniture from the collection of Mary Harris.*

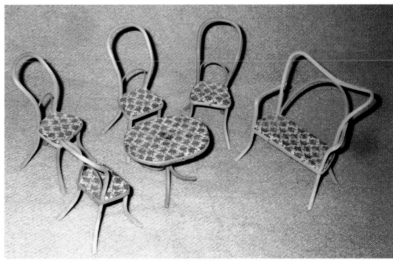

Although this six piece set of large 1" to one foot scale furniture is not marked, it was probably made in Japan. This wicker furniture was produced for many years using different "upholstery" materials. Sometimes fringe was added for decoration.(set $50-75). *Photograph and furniture from the collection of Mary Harris.*

1920s

Even though this wood furniture looks very much like it came from the German Gottschalk line, it was actually made in Japan. The upholstery on the easy chair and settee match. They are stamped with a large "Japan" on the bottoms and are in 1" to one foot scale (set $50+).

Eight piece oak Japanese dining room set of furniture in a 1" to one foot scale, circa late 1920s or early 1930s. The furniture is nicely made with an added leaf for the table. Flowered paper has been used to add decoration to the furniture. The cabinet doors are functional. Each piece of furniture is marked with a sticker stamped "MADE IN JAPAN." The number 528 has been written on the bottom of some of the furniture (set $75).

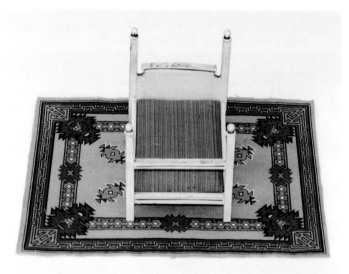

This large 1" to one foot scale wood bed also has a "Gottschalk" look but it is stamped with a small "Japan" mark on the bottom ($50+).

Japanese furniture in original wood box, circa late 1920s. The box can be used as a cabinet. The furniture is finished in black lacquer with added gold designs. The tables are 1.5" tall and 2.25" wide (set $50-75). *Photograph and furniture from the collection of Ruth Petros.*

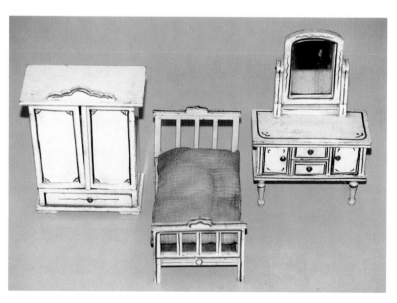

Left:
Japanese wood furniture was also made using a white and gold motif. This set, consisting of a bed, vanity, and wardrobe, carries the small stamped "Japan" mark. A matching ice box (not pictured) is marked with the large "Japan" stamp. The items are 1" to one foot in scale and the doors and drawers are functional. All of this type furniture appears to be circa late 1920s (set $75+).

1930s

Japanese wood dining room set in original box, circa 1930s. The front of the box pictures other rooms of furniture also produced by the unknown firm. The box is marked "Made In Japan" on a paper sticker. The sideboard is 3" high x 4" wide, the table is 4.25" long by 2.75" wide. The wood teacart has metal wheels. See *Antique and Collectible Dollhouses* for a photograph of the boxed "music room." (MIB $95). *Photograph and furniture from the collection of Ruth Petros.*

The design of the bedroom furniture looks very much like that of the 1931 American Schoenhut bedroom pieces pictured on the top row. Besides the vanity and beds, the dresser and chairs also follow the same patterns.

Wood bedroom furniture pictured on the Japanese box to be used for furnishing both bedrooms of the house shown on the box's cover. Each bedroom was supplied with only one bed and either the dresser or vanity and bench and/or chair to be used to complete the furnishings. The furniture is stamped on the bottom in small print "Made in Japan." The drawers are functional. The furniture is a large 3/4" to one foot in scale (set $50+).

No real living room furniture is pictured on the front of the Japanese dining room box but a piano and bench are shown in an upstairs room along with a table and chair. This stamped "Made in Japan" piano and bench is similar to the other flower decorated pieces but is a little smaller in scale ($15).

Wood kitchen pieces shown in the house on the box cover include a table, chair, stove, ice box, and cabinet. This furniture is also in a large 3/4" to one foot scale. The doors and drawers are functional. The stove, ice box, table, and chair are made from a very similar design used by a German manufacturer during this same period. Pictured is the "Made in Japan" stove on the left and the German stove on the right. Although the Japanese pieces are a little larger, the basic designs are very similar.

Several sets of what appears to be Japanese dollhouse furniture were advertised in the Butler Brothers catalog for September 1934. The wholesale prices ranged from 37 cents to $2.00 for a dozen sets of the furniture. *From the collection of Marge Meisinger.*

This boxed set of small scale wicker furniture is similar to the set advertised in the Butler Brothers catalog in 1934. These sets were exported from Japan for many years in a variety of sizes. This sofa is 3.25" wide x 2.25" tall. The bottom of each piece of furniture is stamped "Made in Japan." The box front also carries the "Made in Japan" mark. The original price tag on the box reads 10 cents ($20-25).

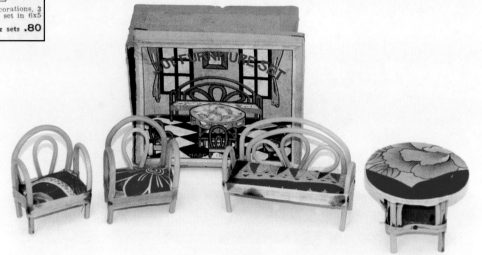

Another similar Japanese wicker set was sold with four colorful bisque dolls sitting in the chairs. The dolls are incised "JAPAN" on their backs. The dolls and chairs are approximately 2" tall. Everything is still tied to the original cardboard ($50-65). *Photograph and item from the collection of Ruth Petros.*

Below:
"Made in Japan" wood table and chairs, circa early 1930s. It is numbered 49096/5 on the box. A cabinet and rocking chair are also pictured but there would have been no room for these extra pieces so perhaps they came in another set. The furniture was made very cheaply. The table is 2.75" high and the chairs are 3.75" tall (set $35). *Photograph and furniture from the collection of Becky Norris.*

Boxed set of Japanese wood bedroom furniture, circa 1930s. The furniture has been finished with hand painted and burnt decorations. It is similar to sets offered in the Butler Brothers catalog in 1934. Dining room, living room, and kitchen sets were also made. The bed is 5" long and the vanity is 4.5" high (MIB $75). *Photograph and furniture from the collection of Ruth Petros.*

This boxed Japanese wood kitchen set matches the bedroom furniture. It, too, carries the hand painted and burnt decorations. The set includes a cabinet 4.5" high x 3" wide, table 4" long, two chairs, and a stove (MIB $75). *Petros Collection.*

Boxed Japanese wood dog house, complete with two china dogs. This house is also hand painted with burnt decorations. 2.5" high x 4" wide (MIB set $35). *Petros Collection.*

Wood playground sets, circa 1930s. The green cat swing is marked "Made in Japan." It is 6.5" high. The red shoofly, teeter totter, slide, swing, and bench are marked "Japan" and came as a set. The swing is 3.5" high and the teeter totter is 5.5" long (cat swing $25+, set $50+). *Petros Collection.*

Boxed Japanese wood furniture with hand painted decorations, circa 1930s. The furniture ranges from 3/4" to 1" to one foot in scale. Most of the pieces are stamped "Made in Japan." The box is also marked "Made in Japan." The floor lamp is very similar to the floor lamps produced by Strombecker and Schoenhut during the 1930s. The doors and drawers are functional ($50+).

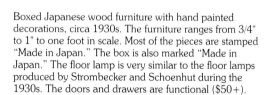
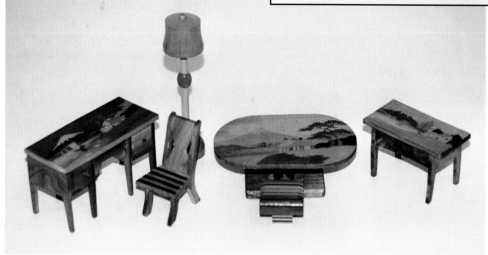

Additional pieces of Japanese wood furniture with slightly different designs. Although the floor lamp is similar, the shade is longer. These pieces are not marked (set $35).

Japanese "Strombecker and Grand Rapids"

In the earlier part of the twentieth century, Japanese craftsman were always very good at copying other firms' designs and marketing them as original products. This wood bedroom set is a very good example. Its design is almost exactly like the 1934 Strombecker 3/4" to one foot scale bedroom furniture. Only the chair front and cut-outs and the addition of the designs on the tops of the furniture make the pieces different. The furniture is marked "Made in Japan." *Photograph and furniture from the collection of Becky Norris.*

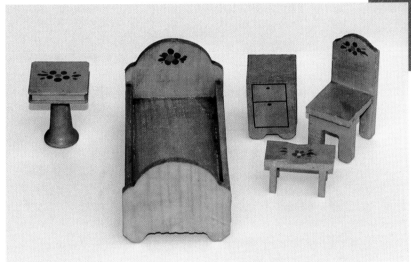

Left:
This marked Japanese bedroom furniture bears a striking resemblance to Strombecker 3/4" to one foot "Modern" furniture from 1938. The bed, chair, and night stand are nearly identical. Even the yellow color is the same. Hand painted flowers and black lines make the sets different (set $25-35).

Below:
Furniture known to collectors as "Grand Rapids" was also copied and marketed by a firm in Japan. The bed and dresser on the top row are American made while the furniture pieces on the bottom row were made in Japan. Living room furniture, based on the American patterns, was also produced and exported by Japan.

Japanese craftsmen continued to copy Strombecker products through the years. Although the radio, chair, and table on the bottom are not marked, it is thought that they were made in Japan. Dining room furniture on the top row was produced by Strombecker. All are in a 1" to one foot scale. A similar table was advertised in the Shackman catalog in 1973 with trussed legs and a beveled top. It was made in Japan using cherry wood.

Decorated Wood Furniture

This trio of small scale wood Japanese tables and chairs represent inexpensive products exported by Japan for decades. The middle set, which features burnt wood designs, is the oldest. The set decorated with large flowers is of more resent vintage (sets $10-15 each). *Photograph and furniture from the collection of Becky Norris.*

China Furniture

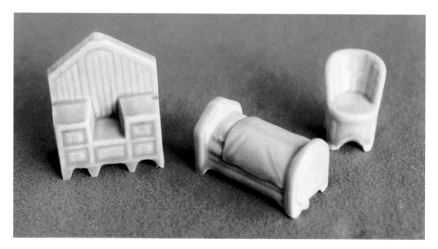

Japanese dresser and chair like those advertised in the 1936 Butler Brothers catalog. Instead of a bed, a stool was the third piece in the catalog set. This china set is marked "Made in Japan" on blue and white stickers. The furniture is in 3/4" to one foot scale (set $35). *From the collection of Gene and Arliss Morris. Photograph by Gene Morris.*

3-Pc. Furniture Sets — China, vory finish with colored floral decorations, 6 styles, kitchen, library, dining, living and bathroom. Each set in box.
64-7880—1 doz sets
n pkg........Doz sets .37

The Butler Brothers fall and winter catalog of 1936 pictures several sets of china furniture "Made in Japan." The three piece sets came in six styles: kitchen, bathroom, library, dining room, living room, and bedroom. A dozen sets sold for 37 cents. This type of furniture was marketed by Japanese firms for many years.

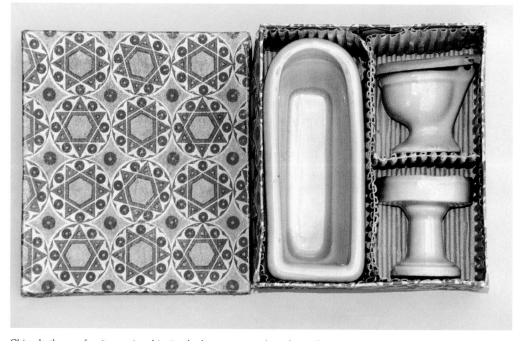

China bathroom furniture using this simple design was made in Japan for many years. This boxed set is marked "The House of Seco Service" as well as "Made in Japan" on the outside of the box. The individual pieces are also stamped "Made in Japan." This set is probably of more recent vintage. The furniture is a large 3/4" to one foot in scale (set $25+).

Boxed china kitchen set, circa 1930, made in Japan for the George Borgfeldt Corp. of New York City. The title on the box reads "Dolly's Kitchen DeLuxe No.85." The set includes a stove, sink, ice box, and cabinet. Each piece was incised "Japan" on the back and is in a large 3/4" to one foot scale. Since the furniture was so breakable, it is surprising that so much of it has survived (MIB $50+).

China dining room furniture in 3/4" to one foot scale, marked "Made in Japan." The set includes a table, four chairs, and a sideboard (set $35). *From the collection of Arliss and Gene Morris. Photograph by Gene Morris.*

The most collectible of the more recent Japanese porcelain furniture are those pieces marked "Made in Occupied Japan." This furniture was produced shortly after World War II. The piano and the lady on the bench are both marked in this manner. Other pieces include a sofa and chair, clock, bench, lamp and table. All of the pieces are in a 3/4" to one foot scale (Occupied Japan pieces $15-20 each, others $5-10 each). *Morris Collection.*

Two china Japanese chairs, lamp, chest, and lady in 3/4" to one foot scale. Each piece carries the "Japan" mark ($8-10 each). *Morris Collection.*

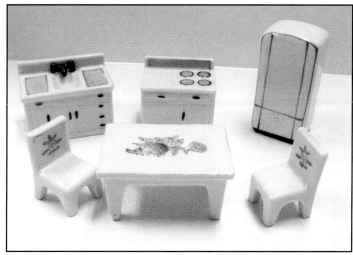

A more recent china kitchen set "Made in Japan." This set includes a sink, stove, refrigerator, table and two chairs (set $35-45). *Furniture from the collection of Judy Mosholder. Photograph by Gary Mosholder.*

Metal Furniture

"Dolly's Drawing Room" boxed set of Japanese furniture, circa 1950s. The metal cuckoo clock is 4" high, table and piano both 2" high. The box is marked "Grace/Made in Japan." The trademark of an Indian's face also appears on the box (set $50). *Photograph and furniture from the collection of Ruth Petros.*

Metal furniture "Made in Japan." The unusual grill is 2.5" high x 2.5" wide and came complete with accessories ($50). The boxed set includes a smaller scale table and two chairs ($25-35), while the unboxed metal table and chairs are in a little larger scale (set $15). *Petros Collection.*

Boxed "Little Mother's Kitchen," circa late 1950s or early 1960s. The box is marked "SSS International/Made in Japan." The set includes pink tin appliances plus a smaller scale table and chairs. Included are a stove, sink, refrigerator, and washing machine. The refrigerator measures 4.75" high (MIB $125). *Petros Collection.*

Boxed Japanese set of metal furniture, circa 1950s. The box is marked "It's Cragstan for Toys." An Indian head trademark, along with "Japan" also appears on the box. The "Dolly's Furniture Set" includes a table and two chairs plus a settee, doll bed, and plastic doll. All of the furniture is in a large 3/4" to one foot scale (MIB set $25-35).

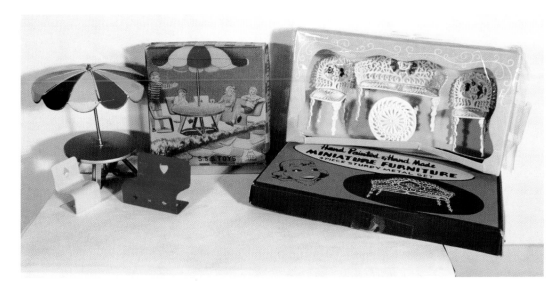

Boxed 1" to one foot scale furniture, circa 1950s. The metal and fabric furniture is still attached to its original cardboard. The set includes a table, two chairs, settee, and a lamp (set $50-75). *Photograph and furniture from the collection of Ruth Petros.*

Two boxed sets of furniture "Made in Japan." The box for the umbrella, table and two chairs is marked "SSS Toys/Japan" and probably dates from the 1950s. The umbrella is 3.5" high (boxed $25). The lightweight white metal furniture is circa 1960s. It includes a table, two chairs, and a settee. The chairs are 2.5" tall (boxed set $25). *Petros Collection.*

Dolls

"Quintette" dolls, made in Japan during the 1930s when the Canadian Dionne Quintuplets were so popular. The painted bisque dolls are 5" tall with molded hair and painted features. They are wearing their original clothing and are in their original box. The dolls are the right age and size to be used with the large scale furniture produced by Schoenhut, Strombecker, and Wisconsin Toy during the 1930s. Each doll is marked "Made in Japan" on her back (Boxed set $125+).

Temple

Traditional Japanese Temple complete with original dolls, including the emperor, his wife, and members of his court. The larger doll on the left has been added to the set ($500 plus $50-75 for the additional doll). 27" high x 20" wide x 14" deep. *Photograph and temple from the collection of Ruth Petros.*

Left:
"White" bisque jointed dolls marked on their backs "Made in Japan," circa 1930s. The 4.5" dolls have molded hair and painted features and are wearing their original clothing. These dolls fit nicely with the large 3/4" to one foot scaled Japanese furniture pictured earlier (Pair $50-75).

Dishes

Hand painted very fine thin porcelain tea set made in "Occupied Japan." The set features hand painted roses with gold trim. The teapot measures 1.25" tall (set $50). *Photograph and tea set from the collection of Ruth Petros.*

Chapter 7
Display

One of the hardest tasks associated with a collection of dollhouses is the never-ending search for places to put them all. Some collectors try to arrange all their houses in one room, perhaps in a finished basement. Others use the houses and furniture as decorative accessories throughout the house. It is hoped that the following photographs will give collectors some new insight to help them answer the question, "Where shall I put it?"

These outdoor items add interest to the railroad station display. The same accessories can be used to enhance the yard of an old dollhouse. Three of the boxes read "Jefferson Sales & Co./Makers of Easy Built Mountain Scenery and Garden Accessories." One of the sundial boxes is labeled "Maurer Paint Co. Toy Division/Philadelphia, Penn./Makers of Easy Built etc." Pictured are a Flag Plot #201, Fountain, Sun Dial #23, and gazing ball. The pieces are made of wood that has been finished with a concrete look. The sundial and "water" in the fountain are metal. All of the accessories are 3/4" to one foot in scale (boxed $30+ each). *Carey Collection*

This antique oak store showcase provides space on top to display a Gottschalk "Red Roof" house. A Schoenhut railroad station and accessories are featured inside the glass covered case. There are sliding glass doors in the back to allow easy access. *Photograph, case, and buildings from the collection of Gail and Ray Carey.*

Pair of German folding deck chairs in 1" to one foot scale. These pieces can be used on a porch or in the yard of a dollhouse when outdoor accessories are needed ($15-20 each). *Carey Collection.*

Gail and Ray Carey also made this shelf, which hangs in a bathroom in their home. Gail's extra pieces of bathroom furniture are displayed on the shelves. *Carey Collection*.

Gail Carey's dollhouse collection features some very large houses. She and her husband Ray made the cabinet that holds this homemade dollhouse. The cabinet doors open to allow access to shelves that can be used to store dollhouse furniture or MIB dollhouse items. *Carey Collection*.

This small dollhouse (made of two cigar boxes) has a prominent place in another collector's bathroom. The house is furnished with small scale metal "Littles" furniture, made by Mattel, Inc. in the early 1980s (see *American Dollhouses and Furniture* for photographs and information on this furniture).

Collector Marilyn Pittman displays several of her kitchen rooms as well as her Dunham's Cocoanut house in her kitchen. *Photograph and rooms from the collection of Marilyn Pittman.*

Collector Bonnie Benson Hanson is pictured with her Sears Model house, circa 1920s. In front of the house, a catalog page shows the Sears house and floor plan. Since the roof is removable, Bonnie furnished the house as a dollhouse. It is displayed on a late 1800s general store milk can scale. *Photograph and items from the collection of Bonnie Benson Hanson.*

Displayed on the wall are three tin kitchens (probably German) dating from the early part of the twentieth century. A two-room German Christian Hacker wood kitchen and pantry fits nicely on top of an antique cupboard. The room box is identified on the bottom with the Christian Hacker mark. It includes original built-in shelves in both rooms. Most of the furniture and accessories are thought to be original. It is circa late 1800s. *Pittman Collection.*

Left:
"Happy Hour" wood furniture, made by Jaymar circa 1933, is displayed in a narrow bookcase that has been wallpapered to give the shelves more of a dollhouse look. The shelves have been furnished as a bathroom, bedroom, living room, dining room, and kitchen. The fireplace is not a Jaymar product (see *Antique and Collectible Dollhouses* to learn more about this furniture). *Photograph and furniture from the collection of Becky Norris.*

Above and left:
This heavy cardboard unit came from a miniature shop and was originally used to display Concord miniatures. It currently houses interesting pieces of plastic Renwal furniture. The backgrounds of the rooms were made from copies of the early Renwal cardboard inserts. Most of the furniture is from the hard-to-find line that featured decorative decals on the pieces. *Photographs and display from the collection of Roy Specht.*

Linda Boltrek likes other antiques as well as old dollhouses. Several of her houses are displayed on antique tables, as is the Gottschalk "Blue Roof" pictured here. Linda also takes advantage of white commercial shelving as do many collectors. *Photograph and houses from the collection of Linda Boltrek.*

Marge Powell has used dark commercial shelving to display many items from her collection. Marge likes toy buildings as well as houses. She holds a cardboard house featured in the "Cardboard" chapter. *Photograph and houses from the collection of Marge Powell.*

Marilyn Pittman displays most of her houses in her dollhouse room. A series of shelves, near the ceiling, have been built around the room to hold many of the houses. Other houses have been placed on lower shelves and the floor of the room. *Photograph and houses from the collection of Marilyn Pittman.*

Arliss and Gene Morris have built shelves in a basement room to house many of the dollhouses in their collection. This method of displaying houses adds color to a basement, in addition to providing storage space for many houses. The metal houses are especially attractive when displayed in this manner. *Photograph and houses from the collection of Arliss and Gene Morris.*

This large shelving unit in Rita Goranson's home was made by her husband. It holds five houses, including a large Rich house on the bottom shelf that is featured in the "American" chapter. *Photograph and houses from the collection of Rita Goranson.*

Most collectors would think that a city dweller, who lives in an apartment, would not have the space to display a collection of dollhouses. George Mundorf has met the challenge by placing the shelves to hold his dollhouses near the ceiling. Using this method, his collection doesn't interfere with the floor or lower wall space. Many of his houses are displayed in this manner. *Photograph and houses from the collection of George Mundorf.*

Roy Specht's very large dollhouse collection is housed mainly in his garage. The houses are displayed on various tables and shelves in the big open space. Like most dedicated collectors, however, Roy is also running out of room for additional houses. *Photograph and houses from the collection of Roy Specht.*

Because doll houses are so large, miniature museums have difficulty in finding enough room to display their collections. This "street" of mostly Gottschalk "Blue Roof" houses, located at Angel's Attic, is one way for a museum to feature several large houses in a limited space. Private collectors can also adapt this idea if they have space for a deep shelf that would allow the placement of trees and other outdoor accessories. *From the collection of Angel's Attic, Santa Monica, California (310-394-8331). Photograph by Jeff Carey.*

The Dollhouse and Miniature Museum of Cape May uses a variety of methods to display the houses in its collection. Besides white shelving, glass cases and tables are also used for dollhouse display. The museum was opened in 1998 by Libby Goodman in Cape May, New Jersey (609) 884-6371. *Photograph and houses from the collection of the Dollhouse and Miniature Museum of Cape May.*

The Mineral Point Toy Museum, located in Mineral Point, Wisconsin (608) 987-3160, is pleased to be able to display "The Essex House," formerly in the Catherine Dorris Callicott collection. The Callicott collection is featured in the book *In Praise of Dollhouses*, published in 1978. The five-room house is open in the back. The owner of the museum, Carol Stevenson, is pictured with the house. *Photograph and house from the collection of Mineral Point Toy Museum.*

Bibliography

Ackerman, Evelyn. *The Genius of Moritz Gottschalk*. Annapolis, MD: Gold Horse Publishing, 1994.

Adams, Margaret, ed. *Collectible Dolls and Accessories of the Twenties and Thirties from Sears, Roebuck and Co.* New York: Dover Publications, 1986.

Block House, Inc. Catalogs 1940, 1950, 1977. New York: Block House, Inc.

Brett, Mary. *Tomart's Price Guide to Tin Litho Doll Houses and Plastic Doll House Furniture*. Dayton, OH: Tomart Publications, 1997.

Cooper, Patty, and Dian Zillner. *Toy Buildings 1880-1980*. Atglen, PA: Schiffer Publishing Ltd., 2000.

Children's Activities Magazine. Chicago: Child Training Association, Inc. Various Issues 1930s-1950s.

Cieslik, Marianne and Jurgen, eds. *Moritz Gottschalk 1892-1931*. Reprints of Catalog Illustrations. Theriault's Gold Horse Publishing, 2000.

The Doll & Toy Collector. Swansea, England: International Collectors Publications, July/August 1983 and September/October 1983 issues.

Dollhouse and Miniature Collectors Quarterly. Bellaire, MI. Advertisements reprinted in various issues, 1990-1996.

Dolly Dear Accessories. Rives, Tennessee: Dolly Dear, 1958.

Dol-Toi Products. Catalog 1964-5. Stamford, England: Dol-Toi, 1964.

Eaton, Faith. *The Ultimate Dolls' House Book*. London: Dorling Kindersley, 1994.

Grandmother Stover's Doll House Accessories. Columbus, OH: Grandmother Stover, 1977.

Hall's Lifetime Toys Catalog. Chattanooga, Tennessee. Various issues.

International Dolls House News. Leicester, England: Lexus Special Interests. Various issues.

Jackson, Valerie. *A Collector's Guide to Doll's Houses*. Philadelphia, PA.: Running Press, 1992.

Jackson, Valerie. *Dollhouses: The Collectors Guide*. Edison, New Jersey: Book Sales, Inc., 1994.

Jacobs, Flora Gill. *A History of Dolls' Houses*. New York: Charles Scribner's Sons, 1965.

Jacobs, Flora Gill. *Dolls' Houses in America*. New York: Charles Scribner's Sons, 1974.

Kernon, Gillian. "Pit-A-Pat." *International Dolls House News*. Leicester, England: Lexus Special Interests, Summer 1986, p. 16.

Keystone Toy Catalog. Boston, Mass: Keystone Mfg. Co., 1942-43 & 1955.

Kohler, Swantje. "C. Moritz Reichel." *International Dolls House News*. Leicester, England: Lexus Special Interests, June-July 1999, pp. 36-39.

King, Constance Eileen. *The Collector's History of Dolls' Houses*. New York: St. Martin's Press, 1983.

MacLaren, Catherine B. *This Side of Yesterday in Miniature*. LaJolla, CA.: Nutshell News, 1975.

Marshall Field & Company Catalogs. Chicago, IL. Various issues.

Mason & Parker Mfg. Co. Catalog 1914. Winchendon, Mass.: Mason & Parker. Reprint: Catalogues of History, Atascadero, California.

Montgomery Ward. Catalogs. Chicago: Montgomery Ward. Various issues from 1923-1980.

Morton E. Converse and Son Company. Catalogs 1915, 1919. Winchendon, Mass.: Morton E. Converse and Son.

Osborne, Marion. *Bartons "Model Homes."* Nottingham, England: By the Author, 29 Attenborough Lane, Chilwell NG9 5JP, 1988.

Osborne, Marion. *Dollhouses A-Z.* Nottingham, England: By the Author, 29 Attenborough Lone, Chilwell NG9 5JP, n.d.

Osborne, Marion. Continuing Series on Tri-ang, Amersham, Tudor Toys, and Others. *Dolls House and Miniature Scene.* West Sussex, England: EMF Publications.

Osborne, Marion. *Lines and Tri-ang Dollhouses and Furniture 1900-1971.* Nottingham, England: By the Author, 29 Attenborough Lane, Chilwell NG9 5JP, 1986.

Osborne, Marion. *Tri-ang Spot-on Dolls House Furniture 1960-1970.* Self published as above.

Schmuhl, Marian. "Pliant Playthings of the Past." *Dolls: The Collectors Magazine.* December 1993, pp. 50-56.

Schwartz, Marvin. *F.A.O. Schwarz Toys Through the Years.* Garden City, New York: Doubleday and Co., Inc., 1971.

Sears, Roebuck and Company Catalogs. Chicago: Sears, Roebuck and Company. Various issues from 1900-1982.

Snyder, Dee. "The Collectables." *Nutshell News,* "Dolly Dear Accessories," July-August 1979; "Exclusive Offering," May 1990; "Mary Frances Line," January 1990.

Theriault, Florence. *Little Houses By the Side of the Road.* Theriault's Gold Horse Publishing, 2001.

Timpson, Anne B. "The Christian Hacker Firm." *International Dolls House News,* Winter 1993, pp.36-39.

Timpson, Anne B. "Rococo Revival by Rock and Graner." *International Dolls House News,* December 1995/January 1996, pp. 39-41.

Towner, Margaret. *Dollhouse Furniture.* Philadelphia, PA.: Running Press, 1993.

The Universal Toy Catalog of 1924/1926 (Der Universal Speilwaren Katalog). Reprint Edition. London: New Cavendish Books, 1985.

Whitton, Blair, ed. *Bliss Toys and Dollhouses.* New York: Dover Publications, Inc., 1979.

Whitton, Blair. *Paper Toys of the World.* Cumberland, MD.: Hobby House Press, Inc.

Whitton, Margaret, ed. *Dollhouses and Furniture Manufactured by A. Schoenhut Company, 1917-1934* (reprinted.)

Wisconsin Toy Company. Catalog circa mid-1930s. Milwaukee, WI: Wisconsin Toy Co. n.d.

Zillner, Dian. *American Dollhouses and Furniture From the 20th Century.* Atglen, PA: Schiffer Publishing Ltd., 1995.

Zillner, Dian. *Furnished Dollhouses 1880s-1980s.* Atglen, PA: Schiffer Publishing Ltd., 2001.

Zillner, Dian, and Patty Cooper. *Antique & Collectible Dollhouses and Their Furnishings.* Atglen, PA: Schiffer Publishing Ltd., 1998.

Index

A

Action Apartment House, 183
Adrian Cooke Metallic Works, 30
Allied Molding Corp., 177
American Colortype Co., 132
American Crayon Co., 133
American Toy & Furniture Co., 95
American Toy Co., 160
American Toy Furniture (Star), 51, 52
American Woman, 134
Amersham Works, Ltd., 85, 197
Amsco, 149
Androscoggin Pulp Co., 140
Andrews, O.B., 129, 143
Arco Industries, Ltd., 183-185
Arista Finest Quality Toys, 172
Art Toy Co., 138
Arts and General Publishers, Limited, 130
Australia Marquis, 172
Austrian Bronze, 39

B

Barton, A. & Co., 65, 104, 105, 200
Benda-Toy, 145
Best Plastics Corporation, 102
Bex Molding, 197
Biedermeier, 5-9, 12, 14-16, 19-22, 24, 25, 27, 46, 50, 201, 207, 208
Bliss, R., 153
Block House, 125
Blondie House, 107, 108
Blue Box Toys, 118
Borgfeldt, George, 229
Bradley's Playhouse Furniture Cut-Outs, 133
Brimtoy, 65
Bristol Glass, 8, 9, 15, 201
Brumberger Company, 119-120
Built-Rite, 129, 142

C

Caco Dolls, 77, 114, 128

Candy Boxes, 38, 195, 209
Cass, N.D., 41, 42
CEL-Met Products, 138
Charbens, 197
Cheerio, 101
Child Guidance, 180
Child Life Toys, Inc., 179
Concord Toy Co., 144
Converse, Morton E., 74, 75
Cragstan, 231
Crescent Toy Co., 200
Cross and Blackwell Foods, 167

D

Dean & Son Limited, 131
Dinky Toys, 195, 196
Dixon Doll House, 147
Dollhouse Dolls, 5-9, 11-13, 16, 17, 20-28, 30-36, 38, 40, 42, 44, 45, 51, 52, 55, 60, 64, 65, 71, 72, 75, 76
Dolly Dear, 77, 97
Dollyhome, 179
Dolly's Cottage, 135
Dolly's Home, 134
Dol-Toi, 104-106, 200
Donna Lee, 166
Douglas Mfg. Co., 134
Durrel Co., 129, 139

E

Eagle Toys Limited, 99-101
East German, 220
Eeserect Foldaway Doll House, 105
Elastolin, 210
Erna Meyer Dolls, 112
Evans & Cartwright, 12, 20, 35, 187

F

Fairylite, 65
Fairy Princess Interlocking Doll Furniture, 133
Famous Corporation, 169

Flagg Doll Co., 103
Florence Stove Co., 146
Fold-away Doll's House, 146
French Metal Furniture, 32, 156, 213
Fretwork Furniture, 28
Frier Steel, 63
Futurland Miniatures, 167

G

Gable House & Carton Co., 129, 137
Gabriel, Sam'l, 130-132
Game Makers Co., 147
German Red Stained Furniture, 49, 214
Golden Oak, 19, 208
Gottschalk, Moritz, 31, 43, 44, 54-62, 201-204, 206, 233
Graham, Charles E., 135
Grandmother Stover, 97
"Grand Rapids," 227
Grimm & Leeds Co., 129, 134

H

Hacker, Christian, 13, 201, 235
Hall's Lifetime Toys, 121-124
Home For Dolly, 150
House We Live In, 131
Hubsch (East Germany), 220
Hugh Specialty Co., 78, 84

I

Ideal Novelty & Toy Co., 102
IMCO, 185, 186

J

Japanese Temple, 232
Jaydon Molds, 178
Jayline Toys, Inc., 129, 148
Jaymar "Happy Hour" Furniture, 150, 236
Jean Plastic Furniture, 217
Jefferson Sales & Co., 147, 233

Jennys Home, 115-117, 194
The Jolly Jump-ups and Their New House, 131

K

Kage Company, 91
Keystone Mfg. Co., 165
Kiddie Brush & Toy Co., 93
Kiddies' Bungalow, 134
Kilgore, 63
Kitty Puppenmobel (West Germany), 218
Kleemann, O. & M., 199
Kleenex House, 148
Korbi, 58

L

Lee Manufacturing, 98
LePageville Houses, 138
Let's Make Furniture, 133
Lincoln Furniture, 160
Lines Bros., 190
Lines, G. & J., 45-50, 189-190
Little Pet's Play House, 130
"Littles" Furniture, 234
Loofah Trees, 47
Lynnfield, 125

M

Macris Company, 78
Magnetic Doll House, 180
Mammoth Doll House, 140
Marklin, 15, 22-24, 38, 207
Mary Mag-Powrs Doll House, 179
Marx, Louis, 107-109, 174-177
Mary Frances, 93, 94
Mason and Parker, 53
Mattel Creations, 167
Mattel, Inc., 234
McLoughlin Brothers, 129, 131
Meccano Ltd., 195, 196
Meet the Family Figurines, 173
Menasha Woodenware Corp., 79, 80
Meritoy Corp., 92
Milton Bradley Co., 133
Miner Industries, 181, 182
Miniaform, 78, 84, 93
Moko, 211
Montgomery Ward House, 164

Mother Goose Toys, 157, 158
Multiple Products Corp., 181, 182
My Doll's House, 131
My Dolly's Home, 130
Mystery House, 18, 19, 21

N

Nancy Ann Story Book Dolls, 79-81, 96
Nancy Forbes, 95
National Playthings, 145
Needlecraft Magazine, 132

O

Ormolu Accessories, 8, 12, 15-17, 19, 23, 25, 37, 38, 205
Our New Home, 130

P

Penny Toy, 62
Peter Pia, 154
Pit-a-Pat, 65, 85, 86, 196
Plasco, 102, 169-172
Playwood Plastics Co. Inc., 173
PMC Limited, 183
Pop-up Dollhouse, 149
Princess Elizabeth's Little House, 131

Q

Quintette Dolls, 232

R

Ralston Industries, 102
Reichel, C. Moritz, 211
REL Manufacturing Corp., 171
Renwal Manufacturing Co., 167-169, 236
Rich Toy Co., 84, 161-163
Rock & Graner, 6, 26, 205, 207
Roger Williams Toys, 154

S

Schoenhut, 96, 156, 157, 233
Schwarz, F.A.O., 18, 37, 75-77, 110-114
Sears Model House, 235

Shackman, B., 126-128
Siber & Fleming type, 186
Sonia Messer, 125
South Bend Toy Mfg. Co. Inc., 149
SSS International, 230
Star – American Toy Furniture, 51, 52
Stecher Litho. Co., 131
Stirn and Lyon, 152
Strombecker, 90, 111, 161, 223, 227
Susy Goose, 93
Sutherland Paper Co., 129, 141

T

Taylor & Barrett, 61
Terre Town Playhouses, 139
Tootsietoy, 53, 155, 156
Toy Makers, 136
Toy Town Furniture, 197
Transogram, 129
Treen, 6, 13, 15, 19, 22, 23
Tri-ang, 50, 64, 65, 115-117, 190-194
Triangtois, 190, 191
Trixytoy, 139
Tynietoy, 66-70

V

Velva Toys, 173
Victory Toy Co., 93, 94

W

Wagner, D.H. & Sohn, 71, 212, 213
Waltershausen, 14, 21
Walton's Dollhouse, 149
Warren Paper Products, 129, 141, 142
Wayne Paper Products, 129
Westacre Village, 195
West German, 216-220
Whitney Reed, 30
Wicker Toy Mfg. Co., 158
Wilder Manufacturing Co., 89
Wilmot Corp., 140
Wisconsin Toy Co., 159
Whitman Publishing Co., 133
Wolverine Toy Co., 187
Woman's Day House, 79, 82, 83
Woodburn Manufacturing Co., 166
Wright, J.L., 160